BOOK 2

BEYOND REASONABLE DOUBT: A GUIDE TO DESIGNING EXPERIMENTS IN THE BEHAVIOURAL SCIENCES

The Open University

This publication forms part of an Open University course SD226 *Biological psychology: exploring the brain*. The complete list of texts which make up this course can be found on the back cover. Details of this and other Open University courses can be obtained from the Student Registration and Enquiry Service, The Open University, PO Box 197, Milton Keynes MK7 6BJ, United Kingdom: tel. +44 (0)845 300 60 90, email general-enquiries@open.ac.uk

Alternatively, you may visit the Open University website at http://www.open.ac.uk where you can learn more about the wide range of courses and packs offered at all levels by The Open University.

To purchase a selection of Open University course materials visit http://www.ouw.co.uk, or contact Open University Worldwide, Walton Hall, Milton Keynes MK7 6AA, United Kingdom for a brochure. tel. +44 (0)1908 858793; fax +44 (0)1908 858787; email ouw-customer-services@open.ac.uk

The Open University
Walton Hall, Milton Keynes
MK7 6AA

First published 2004. Second edition 2006. Reprinted 2007

Edited, designed and typeset by The Open University.

Printed and bound in the United Kingdom by Halstan Printing Group, Amersham.

ISBN 978 0 7492 1431 9

2.2

The paper used in this publication contains pulp sourced from forests independently certified to the Forest Stewardship Council (FSC) principles and criteria. Chain of custody certification allows the pulp from these forests to be tracked to the end use (see www.fsc-uk.org).

SD226 COURSE TEAM

Course Team Chair

Miranda Dyson

Course Managers

Alastair Ewing
Tracy Finnegan

Course Team Assistant

Yvonne Royals

Authors

Saroj Datta
Ian Lyon
Bundy Mackintosh
Heather McLannahan
Kerry Murphy
Peter Naish
Daniel Nettle
Ignacio Romero
Frederick Toates
Terry Whatson

Multimedia

Sue Dugher
Spencer Harben
Will Rawes
Brian Richardson

Other Contributors

Duncan Banks
Mike Stewart

Consultant

Jose Julio Rodriguez Arellano

Course Assessor

Philip Winn (University of St Andrews)

Editors

Gerry Bearman
Rebecca Graham
Gillian Riley
Pamela Wardell

Graphic Design

Steve Best
Sarah Hofton
Pam Owen

Picture Researchers

Lydia K. Eaton
Deana Plummer

Indexer

Jane Henley

Contents

BEYOND REASONABLE DOUBT: A GUIDE TO DESIGNING EXPERIMENTS IN THE BEHAVIOURAL SCIENCES

1.1 Introduction

1.1.1 Why do we need experiments?

Experiments are fundamental to biology, psychology, and indeed, to all areas of science. It is through experiments that observation and anecdote become substantiated as real events or refuted as mistakes or anomalies. It is through experiments that general statements about events, the relationships between those events and the causes that underlie them are tested. For example, suppose someone hears on the radio a mother describing that she is responsible for washing the football strip for the team her son plays for, and how she can always recognize her son's football shirt by its smell. The listener might infer that all mothers can recognize their sons' shirts by smell. They can do an experiment to find out if the general statement that 'a mother can recognize her son's shirt by its smell' is true for other mothers and their sons. If all the mothers they test can recognize their sons' shirts, then the statement would seem to be valid. If only some of the mothers can recognize their sons' shirts then the general statement is not valid and would have to be modified to 'some mothers can recognize their sons' shirts by smell'. Or it may be that the mother on the radio (or her son!) was unusual, and that most mothers cannot recognize their sons' shirts by smell (always assuming that the mother on the radio was using smell and not, inadvertently, using some other cue such as size or a fault in the stitching).

Experiments are used to verify something, sometimes an observation or anecdote, that is presented as a general statement, or an hypothesis, a term we consider in a later section. These experiments can take one of a number of different forms. They may involve questionnaires, where people tick boxes to agree or disagree with printed statements. They may involve interviews, where people are questioned about their feelings or motives. A comprehensive consideration of all forms of experiments and their associated techniques is not possible in this short course, though further examples and a consideration of the scientific process are presented in Book 3, Chapter 2. Neither is it possible to discuss what is done with those observations that cannot be turned into experiments, for example differences in disease susceptibility or the effects of trauma. What follows then is a detailed examination of one form of experiments, not a comprehensive account of experimentation. The form of the experiments that are described in this book largely concern a variable that can be manipulated.

In the next section, several key terms, including 'variable', are introduced.

1.1.2 Variables and data

To generate a personal sleep record you would have to measure sleep duration and you would measure it by timing it. The measurements you record would be your

data. The word data is plural. If you measured how long you slept on one night, you would have one *datum*; if you measured sleep duration over several nights you would have some data. Such data can be quite interesting; they can reveal patterns such as sleep duration on nights six and seven being longer than for the rest of the week. It is also possible to apply summary statistics to these data, such as *average* sleep duration and *modal* sleep onset latency. (Sleep onset latency is the time between initial eye closure and sleep beginning.) Such observations are an important part of behavioural science, but they do not constitute an experiment. To see why this is so, look at the sleep data in Figure 1.1.

The data in Figure 1.1 were taken from a single person, called a **participant** (in some texts they are called observers or subjects). Participants have their data recorded, as opposed to experimenters who actually record the data. The participant in this case wore a wristband that continuously monitored wrist movement. The wrist movement data were transmitted to a computer that recorded periods of no wrist movement as sleep and periods of wrist movement as awake.

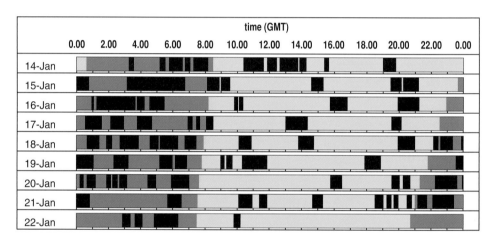

Figure 1.1 Sleep records over nine consecutive 24-hour periods. The black bars indicate sleep; blue areas are night-time; yellow areas are daytime.

◆ Look at Figure 1.1 and briefly describe the sleep pattern. In particular, what two things strike you as unusual about the record?

◆ There are lots of relatively short bursts of sleep lasting about an hour or so, scattered throughout each 24-hour period, perhaps with a preponderance of sleep at night. The two things that might have struck you as unusual are (a) the interrupted nature of the sleep and (b) the amount of sleep during the day.

◆ Drawing on your general knowledge of sleep patterns and of the sleep patterns of people you know or know about, make a note of any groups of people from whom you think the participant could have been taken, e.g. postal workers, soldiers on manoeuvres, new parents.

◆ New parents is one possibility, as is new babies. You might have thought of the very old or those suffering from a sleep disorder, such as narcolepsy. (Narcolepsy is considered in Book 3, Chapter 2.)

In fact, the data are those of the lone, round-the-world yachtswoman, Ellen MacArthur.

The point of this exercise is what it reveals about variables and variation. **Variables** are things that vary or change from time to time or from participant to participant.

The time at which you go to sleep each night and how long you sleep are both variables. The age of the participant and whether the participant has given birth recently are both variables. Weight, height, extent of hair loss, number of teeth, alcohol consumption and number of Open University courses studied are all variables. A variable may come in different forms, as with types of cell, or may have different values, as with sleep duration. A variable is quite simply something that is not always the same, something that varies. **Variation** is the extent to which participants differ on a particular variable, such as sleep duration. The variable is the thing you are interested in; the variation is the range of values the variable can take.

◆ From the data in Figure 1.1, what is the range of variation in number of sleep episodes in the 24-hour periods?

◆ The *smallest* number of sleep episodes is 4 on the 22nd January and the *largest* number of sleep episodes is 12 on the 18th January.

Participants differ on a particular variable not just between each other, but also from time to time. Ellen's sleep pattern and sleep duration differ from one day to the next. Your sleep pattern as an adult probably comprises one long period of sleep every 24 hours, whereas your sleep pattern as a baby was more likely to comprise several short periods of sleep every 24 hours. Your sleep pattern as an infant was probably different again, with one long and one short period of sleep. Age is an inherent property of the participant and, as we have seen, age affects sleep patterns. So variation arises from inherent properties of the participants. In addition, variation can arise from the environment surrounding the participant. The data in Figure 1.1 are not Ellen MacArthur's normal sleep pattern, but those when she was under extreme conditions, alone at sea. The particular environment of single-handed sailing affects her sleep pattern. On land she reverts to a more normal pattern of sleep.

Observing and recording variation may be interesting, but what behavioural and neuroscientists really want to be able to do is establish relationships between variables.

◆ What relationship between what two variables was considered in the previous two paragraphs?

◆ You may have mentioned the fact that the variable 'sleep pattern' alters with the variable 'age'. Alternatively, you may have mentioned the fact that the variable 'sleep pattern' alters with the variable 'environment'.

The general statement, that sleep pattern alters with age or sleep pattern alters with environment, provides the basis for an experiment. Notice that from the vast array of possible variables, two relevant variables have been selected to form the basis of the general statement. What you do in an experiment is to change one variable and see what happens to another variable. That is, experimenters deliberately choose the values or levels of one variable – this variable is *manipulated* – and look to see if this produces corresponding changes in the other variable – the other variable is *measured*. If it does, and there is no further variable in the situation that may have produced the effect, it is assumed the variable manipulated has indeed produced the change observed. This is the logic of experimental design.

For instance, in an experiment to test the general statement 'eating chocolate leads to headaches', one variable would be manipulated, and the other measured. Participants would eat a lot, a little or no chocolate on different occasions and the incidence of headaches would be recorded.

◆ Which variable was manipulated and which variable was measured?

◆ The variable 'chocolate intake' was manipulated and the variable 'incidence of headache' was measured.

Consider another general statement 'rats will stand on their back legs when they hear a click'.

◆ In an experiment to test this general statement, which variable would you manipulate and which variable would you measure?

◆ The variable 'click' (or sound) would be manipulated and the variable 'standing' (or posture) would be measured.

The variable that is manipulated, that is given different values by the experimenter, is called the **independent variable**. The variable that is measured, that is looked at to see if there are any changes produced by the manipulation of the independent variable, is called the **dependent variable**. The dependent variable, therefore, is the variable that shows whether there is any effect of different values of the independent variable. If there is such an effect, then the values that the dependent variable takes will *depend* on the value the experimenters set *independently* for the independent variable.

Experimenters only manipulate the values of the independent variable; they have no direct control over the values taken by the dependent variable. These latter values are obtained from the participants, for example sleep duration, reaction times (e.g. in milliseconds), number of errors made, or number of headaches.

A properly designed experiment will ensure that the relationship between particular variables is established with a fair amount of certainty, or, put another way, that the data generated lead to valid inferences. Setting up an experiment to ensure that the data generated lead to valid inferences is the subject of the next section.

1.1.3 Averages

Averages are an arithmetic way of summarizing data. It is difficult to think about a string of numbers, which is the usual form taken by the data generated in an experiment. However, that string of numbers can be summarized into one number, which is the average. Averages are easy to think about, and they allow simple comparisons to be made as to whether one set of data is greater or smaller than another set. There are two important things to remember about averages. First, they are summaries, and inevitably summaries mask trends and variation. Second, there are different ways of working out the average, each of which can yield a different picture of the data.

The most familiar arithmetic way of summarizing data is the **mean**. The mean is calculated by adding together all the data in a group and dividing the total by the number of items. When people talk about the average, they are usually referring to the mean. Here is an example. The data are the number of people spoken to at the school gates by seven parents one day in spring.

Parent number	1	2	3	4	5	6	7
No. of conversations with different people	4	2	2	9	6	2	2

To calculate the mean number of people spoken to by each parent, find the total number of people spoken to (i.e. $4 + 2 + 2 + 9 + 6 + 2 + 2 = 27$) and divide by the number of items, parents in this case (i.e. 7). The mean is $27/7 = 3.86$. The mean is a very useful summary statistic but you should be aware of two problems. The most important of these is that the mean is influenced by very large or very small values. This is most easily understood in the context of average earnings. Suppose five people each earned £10 000 in a year, four people each earned £20 000 and one other person earned £250 000.

◆ Calculate the mean earnings of the ten people.

◆ The total earnings are $(5 \times £10\,000)$ plus $(4 \times £20\,000)$ plus £250 000, which is £380 000. Divide that figure by the number of items (10 in this case), which gives a mean earnings of £38 000.

The one high value is said to distort the mean. Note that there are nine people with earnings less than the mean and only one with earnings greater than it, so that the summary value, the mean, is not a good guide to average earnings.

The second problem with the mean is that it is arithmetic and you may end up with a mean value that does not make sense in terms of the item being measured. For instance, in the parents' example, the mean was 3.86; but it is not possible to have 0.86 of a conversation. (You may be familiar with the often-quoted figure of 2.4 for the mean number of children in families in the UK.)

The problem of the distortion caused by very high or very low values is overcome by using the median. The median too is a summary statistic but it is unaffected by unusually high or low values. The **median** is found by ranking the values, i.e. putting them in numerical order, starting with the lowest and progressing through to the highest. That value which occupies the middle rank is the median. Here are the conversation data presented in rank form:

Number of conversations	2	2	2	2	4	6	9
Rank	1	2	3	4	5	6	7

The middle rank is 4 (there are three ranks above it and three ranks below). The median number of conversations is therefore the value at rank 4, i.e. 2. Where there is an even number of ranks, the median is the sum of the values at the middle two ranks, divided by two. For example, if there are 12 ranks, the two middle ranks are 6 and 7. The sum of the values at ranks 6 and 7, divided by two, therefore gives the median.

◆ Calculate the median earnings figure for the ten people mentioned earlier in the earnings data.

◆ Rank the data and then find the middle two ranks, which for ten items are 5 and 6. The value at rank 5 is £10 000, and the value at rank 6 is £20 000. Add these values together and divide by two. This gives £10 000 + £20 000 = £30 000; £30 000 ÷ 2 = £15 000. The median earnings figure of the ten people is £15 000.

The other summary statistic is the mode. The mode overcomes both of the problems of the mean, namely the distortion caused by a few very high or very low values and the peculiar values a mean may have. The disadvantage of the mode is that any set of data may have more than one mode. The **mode** is simply that value in the data that occurs most frequently.

◆　What is the mode for the number of conversations?

◆　The value that occurs most frequently is 2; the mode is therefore 2.

◆　What is the mode for the earnings of the ten people?

◆　The value that occurs most frequently is £10 000; the mode is therefore £10 000.

You have probably noticed that the mean, median and mode values for the data in this section are different. So how do you choose between them? Is one a better summary statistic than the other? Choosing between them is a matter of judgement based on how you want to present the data. As a rule of thumb, the median should normally be used if the data include unusually high, or low, values. However, the mean is the preferred summary statistic in the social sciences. There is a right and wrong summary statistic to use for particular types of data, but the distinction need worry only statisticians. For the purposes of this course, you should use either the median or the mean. (When you analyse data using the statistical test described in Section 1.6, you should use the mean.)

The average, whether mean, median or mode, is a single figure, a summary statistic. The observations making up a set of data are scattered on either side of the average, but the average value does not reveal how far the data are spread out. A useful measure of this scatter, or spread, is the range. The **range** is usually presented in brackets after a median and consists of the lowest and the highest observed value of the dependent variable, or sometimes the difference between the lowest and highest observed values.

◆　What would the range of the conversation data be?

◆　The range would be from 2, the lowest datum, to 9, the highest datum, i.e. (2 – 9) or a difference of 7.

An alternative statistic to the range, and the one that should be used in conjunction with the mean, is the variance. The **variance** takes account of the pattern of observed values, not just the two extreme values. It is based on the idea that it is the size of the deviation of each observed value from the mean value that is important. The more observed values that are a long way from the mean (i.e. the greater the spread of data), the higher the variance will be. Conversely, the more observed values that are close to the mean, the lower the variance will be. The variance is calculated by taking the difference between each observed value and the mean, and then multiplying that difference by itself (i.e. squaring the difference). Each of the squared differences is then added together to produce something called the sum of squares. The sum of squares is then divided by one less than the number (n) of observed values ($n - 1$) and the resulting figure is the variance, usually denoted by s^2.

The formula for calculating the variance is therefore as follows (Σ or sigma means 'the sum of'):

$$s^2 = \frac{\sum (\text{mean} - \text{value})^2}{(n-1)}$$

The variance can be quite a large figure and seemingly out of proportion to the mean value – in a sense it is more similar to the square of the mean than to the mean itself. To redress the balance, the square root of the variance is often used as the measure of spread of the data. The square root of the variance, i.e. s, is called the **standard deviation**, sometimes denoted as SD. Where a mean and a standard deviation have been calculated for a set of data, they are usually presented as mean ± SD (e.g. 18 ± 4.2).

Summary of Section 1.1

A variable is anything that can take different values. In experiments, a specific variable is manipulated to see what effect this has on other variables. The manipulated variable is called the independent variable. The variable that is measured in an experiment to see if manipulation of the independent variable has caused any changes is called the dependent variable.

Data may be summarized using the mean, median or mode. The mean is the most commonly used summary statistic, but when a set of data contains an unusually high or unusually low value, the median should be used in preference to the mean. The scatter or spread of the observed values about the median can be indicated by the range. The scatter or spread of the observed values about the mean can be quantified by the standard deviation.

1.2   The experiment

1.2.1   Experimental and control conditions

The simplest experiment involves two values or settings for the independent variable. The different values or settings of the independent variable are called **conditions** and so the simplest experiment comprises two conditions. The dependent variable is then measured under the two conditions to see if the different levels of the independent variable lead to any corresponding differences in the dependent variable. The experiment allows the participants' performance under the two conditions to be directly compared.

For example, this 'two conditions' design could be used to test whether drinking a warm malted beverage at bedtime promotes sleep.

◆   What would the two conditions be?

◆   In one condition the participants would drink a bedtime malted beverage, in the other condition the participants would not drink a bedtime malted beverage.

The manipulation of the independent variable in this case involves the presence of the beverage (in the participant's body; condition 1) and the absence of the beverage (from the participant's body; condition 2). If the malted beverage does promote sleep then participants in condition 1 should sleep better than those in condition 2. If the malted beverage does not promote sleep then there should be no such difference.

There are particular names for the conditions in an experiment where the independent variable is manipulated to indicate its presence and its absence. The condition in which the independent variable is present is called the **experimental condition**. The condition in which the independent variable is absent is the **control condition**. In general, a control condition is one that is *identical in every way* to the experimental condition *except that the independent variable is absent*. Thus, any difference in participants' performance between experimental and control conditions should be due to the effect of the independent variable.

Experiments in which a control condition is compared with an experimental condition can be effective and simple ways to test general statements. However, such a design does not exhaust the possibilities. It may, for instance, be more interesting to compare the effects of two different levels of the independent variable than to compare its presence with its absence. For instance, a drinks company might be more interested in comparing different strengths of malted beverage on sleep patterns. In such an experiment, a malted beverage would be present in *both* conditions; the experiment would have two experimental conditions rather than one experimental and one control condition.

Such a design is perfectly acceptable. In fact, experiments need not be restricted to two experimental conditions; there may be three or more experimental conditions. And there could also be a control condition; that is, a condition in which the variable of interest is absent, if required. So the bedtime drink experiment could consist of participants drinking high strength, medium strength, low strength or a 'no malt' beverage.

◆ In the experiment just described, how many conditions are there and how many of them are experimental conditions?

◆ There are four conditions; three of them are experimental conditions (those in which the beverage is of one of the three different strengths).

There is no 'correct' number of conditions, but when deciding how many conditions to include, two points should be born in mind:

(i) simplicity is often best; don't include more conditions than are necessary.

(ii) the choice of conditions depends on what you need to know; is it important to know what happens in the absence of the independent variable, for instance.

1.2.2 Experimental and null hypotheses

In an experiment then, the independent variable is manipulated by altering the values it takes. The effect of each value of the independent variable, or condition, on the dependent variable is measured. Of critical interest is the effect, if any, that the manipulation of the independent variable has on the dependent variable, so the data generated in one condition are compared with data generated in another condition. Now it is possible to anticipate or hypothesize what the outcome will be, *before* any measurements have been taken. This is a fundamental feature of experimenting and it needs to be considered in some detail.

The outcome of the original malted beverage and sleep experiment has already been considered. It was that if the malted beverage does indeed promote sleep, the participants in the experimental condition (i.e. with the beverage) should sleep more (or better, or get to sleep more quickly, depending on how the dependent variable is defined) than those in the control condition (i.e. without the beverage). If the malted beverage does not affect sleep, then no such difference would be expected.

◆   There is a third possible outcome. What is it?

◆   The third possibility is that the malted beverage impairs sleep.

These three options are the only possible outcomes for experiments involving one experimental and a control condition. Thus, and this is important, it is possible to specify *in advance* what the outcome of the experiment might be.

There is an important distinction to be made between these three potential outcomes. Two of them predict that there will be a difference between the two conditions in sleep. These are the outcomes that would be anticipated if the malted beverage affects sleep in some way (either by promoting or suppressing it). The third outcome is that there will be no noteworthy difference in sleep between the two conditions. This is what would be expected if the malted beverage has no influence on sleep.

Thus if the malted beverage does affect sleep in some way, a different outcome would be predicted, or hypothesized, from what would be expected if the malted beverage did not affect sleep. So, if it is assumed that the malted beverage in some way changes the duration of sleep, it can be hypothesized that there will be a difference in sleep duration between the conditions. And of course the assumption that a malted drink affects sleep, is the same general statement that led to the experiment in the first place. So under this assumption it would be predicted that a difference of some sort would be found between the two conditions. This prediction is called the **experimental hypothesis**. In fact:

(i)   All experiments have experimental hypotheses.

(ii)   Experimental hypotheses *always* predict a difference between conditions, i.e. they predict a difference in the dependent variable as a result of manipulating the independent variable.

But what of the third possible outcome, the prediction that there will be no difference between the two conditions? This is an important prediction and takes a name of its own. It is called the hypothesis of no difference, or the **null hypothesis** (null = amounting to nothing) and it plays a crucial role in the analysis of the experimental data. In fact:

(i)   All experiments have a null hypothesis.

(ii)   The null hypothesis is always the same. It is the prediction that there will be no difference in the dependent variable as a result of manipulating the independent variable.

The null hypothesis is the prediction based on the assumption that the independent variable does not affect the dependent variable. It is a critical hypothesis because, at the end of the experiment, following the analysis of the data, a decision needs to be made. That decision will determine the actual outcome of the experiment, and it takes the form of whether to accept the null hypothesis or reject it. (This decision making process is returned to in Section 1.5.)

Because the null hypothesis plays such a crucial role in deciding the outcome of an experiment it is very important that it is not confused with the experimental hypothesis. The null hypothesis always predicts no difference.

Strictly speaking, the experimental and null hypotheses are to do with statistics rather than experiments. Nonetheless, they provide an important check, when planning an experiment, that the data can be analysed. When planning an experiment, the experimental and null hypotheses should always be stated in terms of the independent and dependent variables.

Before leaving this section there is another aspect of the experimental hypothesis that needs to be considered. The experimental hypothesis can predict not just a difference but also the direction of the difference. For example, in the eating chocolate and headaches experiment (towards the end of Section 1.1.2) the experimenter can be reasonably sure that eating chocolate will either increase the incidence of headaches or have no effect on the incidence of headaches. The experimental hypothesis can reflect this most likely outcome:

'Eating chocolate increases the incidence of headaches'.

◆   What would the corresponding null hypothesis be?

◆   Eating chocolate does not affect the incidence of headaches.

The experimental hypothesis in this case is known as a **directional** (or one-tailed) **hypothesis**, because it predicts an effect in a particular direction. The experimenter who uses a directional hypothesis is simply not interested in a result that goes in the opposite direction. For example, if the directional, experimental hypothesis in the malted beverage experiment had been 'A malted beverage at bedtime will increase the duration of the subsequent night's sleep', then unless the data go in the predicted direction and allow the null hypothesis to be rejected, the experimenter has to accept the null hypothesis. And the null hypothesis in this case would be 'A malted beverage at bedtime has no effect on the duration of the subsequent night's sleep'. Because of this inability to distinguish between no effect and a result that goes in the opposite direction to that predicted, the directional hypothesis should be used with caution. Far more useful is the experimental hypothesis that clearly states there will be a difference between the two conditions, but without specifying the direction. Such an hypothesis is called a **bi-directional** (or two-tailed) **hypothesis.**

◆   State a bi-directional hypothesis for the chocolate/headaches experiment.

◆   Eating chocolate affects the incidence of headaches.

The bi-directional hypothesis allows the experimenter to look for an effect, even if the experimenter is uncertain whether the independent variable will increase or decrease the participants' performance.

1.2.3   Extraneous and confounding variables

In any experiment, in addition to the independent variable and the dependent variable, there will inevitably be other variables which may not be relevant to the current experiment but which are present nevertheless. These additional and unwanted variables are called **extraneous variables**. Extraneous variables include *all* variables other than the independent and dependent variables. For example, in the sleep/malted beverage experiment the amount of exercise taken during the day, or the amount of stress incurred, or the sleep patterns of a participant's family are all variables which could influence the sleep of a participant, and are all variables which are present during the experiment. One of the main aims of experimental design is to ensure that extraneous variables such as these do not interfere with the interpretation of the results. Such interference arises in two different ways. The first and most obvious way is if the extraneous variable renders the data collected meaningless. For example, in the sleep experiment, if the participants were all 'on-call', they could be woken at any time to do their job, rendering their sleep data of no value. This is why experiments are often done in laboratories or under controlled conditions, to ensure the data are as meaningful as possible. However, even under controlled conditions, the second type of interference can occur. The second type of interference arises whenever an extraneous variable is allowed to vary *systematically* along with the independent variable. What this means is that changes in the independent variable are accompanied by changes in an extraneous variable. In this case the extraneous variable introduces *systematic* bias and is said to be a **confounding variable**. If confounding variables are not eliminated from experiments, the data cannot be interpreted because it is not possible to be sure that any effects on the dependent variable are caused by the independent variable rather than by the confounding variable. For instance, in the chocolate and headaches experiment, if the chocolate was always part of a chocolate biscuit, then there would be no way of knowing whether the chocolate or the biscuit had the effect on the incidence of headaches. This is why it is vital to ensure that extraneous variables do not become confounding variables, or, in other words, that *only* the independent variable varies systematically from condition to condition. This can be done by controlling for them, and/or by randomization, and/or by matching participants.

Controlling extraneous variables means ensuring that they do not vary from condition to condition. This can be done in one of two ways. The first way is to eliminate the extraneous variable. Using the chocolate and headaches example where the chocolate is available as chocolate biscuits, the extraneous variable of the biscuit could be eliminated by providing chunks of chocolate instead of chocolate biscuits. The second way of controlling extraneous variables is to ensure that they do not vary from condition to condition. Again, using the chocolate and headaches example, the extraneous variable 'biscuit' could be constant between conditions; the participants in the experimental condition would receive a chocolate biscuit, whilst the participants in the control condition would receive the biscuit *minus* the chocolate.

Controlling extraneous variables works reasonably well for identifiable variables that are external to the participants, e.g. temperature, sound, food availability, etc., but is less effective when the extraneous variables are unknown, or are intrinsic to the participants. Intrinsic variables such as habits, preferences, hygiene products used, etc., may be unknown to the experimenter, and, even if known, may also be difficult to change without affecting the participants. For example, controlling nicotine levels in participants by eliminating smoking and using nicotine patches may have adverse effects on those participants who habitually smoke, because their habits have to change. Alternatively, making all participants consume a certain amount of nicotine may have adverse effects on those who have no experience of nicotine. Such a procedure also raises ethical questions about the rights of participants. (Ethical questions are considered in Book 3, Chapter 2.)

To reduce the possibility of uncontrolled or unknown variables (e.g. those intrinsic to the participants) being confounding, randomization can be used. Randomization relies on the fact that although extraneous variables will inevitably be present in any experiment, they will not vary systematically from condition to condition if care is taken to assign participants randomly to each condition. The word randomization in this context does not mean haphazard. Rather, **randomization** means that appropriate procedures have been used to ensure that the allocation of participants to the conditions is random, meaning that all outcomes are equally likely. For example, one randomization procedure uses a six-sided die. The condition to which participant 1 is allocated is determined by rolling the die. If the number shown is even, participant 1 is allocated to condition 1, if the number shown on the die is odd, participant 1 is allocated to condition 2. The procedure is repeated for each participant. Alternatively, it is sometimes possible to *match* participants. In a situation where, say, some participants were smokers and others were not, systematic bias between conditions in the variable smoking, could be eliminated by matching. Each non-smoker in condition 1 would be paired with, or matched with a non-smoker in condition 2. Similarly, each smoker in condition 1 would be paired with a smoker in condition 2. Strictly speaking, it is the data that are matched; data from participant 1 in condition 1 are always compared with data from the matched participant in condition 2, and likewise for all other participants (see Section 1.3.5).

The important point is that extraneous variables, though present, must not become confounding variables and this is achieved by preventing systematic variation in extraneous variables.

Summary of Sections 1.2.1 to 1.2.3

An experiment requires the dependent variable to be measured under at least two different settings of the independent variable. The different settings of the independent variable are the conditions. The independent variable is present in all the experimental conditions and is absent from the control condition. The effect of the independent variable on the dependent variable can be broadly predicted, and the prediction is called an hypothesis. The hypothesis where the independent variable is predicted to have an effect on the dependent variable is the experimental hypothesis; the hypothesis where the independent variable is predicted to have no effect on the dependent variable is the null hypothesis. Where a difference in the dependent variable is predicted, without specifying whether it might be an increase or a decrease, the experimental hypothesis is bi-directional; where either an increase or a decrease in the dependent variable is predicted, the experimental hypothesis is directional. Confounding variables are those extraneous variables that vary systematically with the independent variable. To ensure that extraneous variables do not become confounding, randomization is often used in the allocation of participants to conditions.

1.2.4   Blind trials

This section continues the theme of controlling extraneous variables, but deals with the situation where the extraneous variable is the experimenter. The first problem to be addressed is that the experimenter might unwittingly treat participants in the different conditions in different ways. For example, if the experiment was testing whether breathing in extra oxygen improved learning, the experimenter might, inadvertently and subtly, act more positively towards participants receiving oxygen-enriched air, than to participants receiving normal air. The positive attitude of the experimenter might engender a positive attitude in the participants in the experimental group, with consequent effects on their performance.

◆ Why would this extraneous variable of positive attitude need to be controlled?

◆ Because the extraneous variable would introduce systematic bias. The experimenter has a positive attitude only to the participants in the experimental condition, so it is a confounding variable.

Another example could be in a different experiment where the experimenter might be more sympathetic towards those participants about to experience pain in the absence of pain relief, i.e. in the control group, than to participants in the experimental group who will receive the pain relief drug under trial. To ensure the equal treatment of all participants, the person administering the independent variable should not know, i.e. should be 'blind', to which condition any particular participant belongs. This is called a **blind trial**.

◆ Computers are very often used to present visual and auditory stimuli to participants. Apart from convenience, what other particular advantage does computer presentation offer?

◆ Computers are not biased; all participants will be presented with the stimuli in exactly the same way. In this context, computers can be considered to be 'blind'.

An added advantage of the blind trial is that it reduces the likelihood that the participants will know to which condition they belong. This is important because it reduces the conscious expectation of an effect.

◆ By what is an effect that is the result of conscious expectation better known?

◆ It is better known as the placebo effect (Book 1, Chapter 1, Section 1.1.7).

The placebo effect is a potential experimental contaminant in many situations. Consider the oxygen and learning experiment above. Participants who know they have received the oxygen-enriched air may perform better, *just because they know they should*, whilst participants who received the normal air may perform indifferently, for the same reason. The oxygen may have no effect at all, but knowledge that they have received oxygen (or not) may be sufficient to change behaviour. Consider another example, the 'Does eating chocolate cause headaches?' experiment. Those eating the chocolate will know they are in the chocolate condition and this knowledge, of itself, may be sufficient to induce a headache. Those participants in the no-chocolate condition will know they have not eaten chocolate so will suffer neither knowledge-induced, nor chocolate-induced headaches. The placebo effect is very powerful in certain contexts.

Participants may learn about the conditions in the experiment and to which condition they belong during the administration of the independent variable. As such knowledge may generate a placebo effect, it is very important to ensure that the person administering the independent variable does not give any clues to the participant as to which condition of the experiment they belong. In other words, all the participants must be treated in exactly the same way before the experiment. And the best way to achieve that is for the experiment to be a blind trial.

The problem discussed above was that of the experimenter unwittingly treating participants in the different conditions in different ways. A second problem, addressed below, is that of the experimenter unwittingly recording the performance of participants in the different conditions in different ways. Again, there is no question of deliberate falsification of data; the issue is one of inadvertent bias. For example, suppose a particular exercise regime was intended to improve posture. When posture was recorded at the end of the experiment the experimenter might err on the side of improvement when scoring posture in experimental participants, e.g. recording 7 for a posture that would have scored 6 for a control participant. Alternatively, knowing such bias to be present, the experimenter might over-compensate and do the opposite, i.e. record 6 for a posture in the experimental group that would have scored 7 in the control group. There are two aspects to this problem, both of which need to be addressed to overcome it.

First, to ensure that the dependent variable is accurately recorded it must be defined carefully from the outset. Sometimes such definition is straightforward, for example where answers are either right or wrong, or the participants either do or do not achieve a particular task in a set time. But often defining the dependent variable is quite tricky, as with the posture example above, or with improvements to speech. Perhaps, with the chocolate and headaches example, the experimenter is interested in the severity of the headache, not just its presence or absence. Such an experiment would require the careful definition of each grade of severity. (Question 1.3 at the end of this chapter asks you to come up with a dependent variable for the malted beverage experiment.)

Second, in addition to a clear definition of the dependent variable, the person recording the dependent variable should not know, that is, should be blind, to which condition the participant being observed belongs. Their task is to record the performance of each participant as accurately as possible, according to the prescribed definition. And when the recorder does not know to which condition any particular participant belongs, there can be no systematic bias to their records. This is another type of blind trial.

Where both types of blind trial are present in the same experiment, i.e. where neither the experimenter nor the participant knows the details of a given trial, the experiment is said to be *double blind*.

1.2.5   Causal inference

One requirement of a good experiment is that all confounding variables have been removed. If the independent variable is then manipulated, and if there are changes in the dependent variable, it would seem logical to infer that the changes in the independent variable *caused* the changes in the dependent variable. The logic is as follows: the dependent variable changed; the only other known change was the change to the independent variable; therefore the change in the independent variable caused the change in the dependent variable. This logical sequence is a **causal inference**.

Suppose that in a well-designed malted beverage and sleep experiment it was found that all the participants in the experimental condition slept for 20 minutes longer than all the participants in the control condition. It could then be inferred that the malted drink promoted sleep. It is possible then to consider which components of the malted beverage had this effect or whether the malted beverage affected some third factor (e.g. a hormone) and it was this third factor that caused the extra sleep.

In this latter case the malted beverage could be said to be having an *indirect* effect. How would these further studies affect the original conclusion?

The answer is not at all. An experiment carried out at one level (e.g. behavioural) cannot be refuted by an experiment carried out at another level (e.g. hormonal). The second experiment merely adds to the overall picture. It might be found, for instance, that stimulating melatonin release also promotes sleep. (In humans, melatonin is a hormone implicated in the regulation of sleep.) However, the conclusion from the original experiment is still valid. What is important is that the word 'cause' is being used in the experimental sense (to describe the overall conclusion to the experiment) and not in an absolute sense (to describe the definitive cause). Put another way, the conclusion that a malted drink promotes sleep is justified, but it leaves other questions, about why it promotes sleep, unanswered.

1.2.6 Correlations

Sometimes two variables appear to maintain a particular relationship with one another (e.g. a high level of one is associated with a high level of the other; or as one rises so the other falls). A case in point involves the number of small lumps, known as amyloid plaques, found in the brains of people with Alzheimer's disease (shown in Figure 2.23 in Book 1, Chapter 2), and the cognitive impairment, i.e. dementia, symptomatic of Alzheimer's disease. The greater the degree of dementia, the greater is the number of plaques subsequently found at autopsy. This is known as a positive **correlation**. The converse is a negative correlation, where as one variable increases the other variable decreases. An example of a negative correlation is the duration of sleep and age. As age increases, so the duration of sleep decreases (see Figure 1.2).

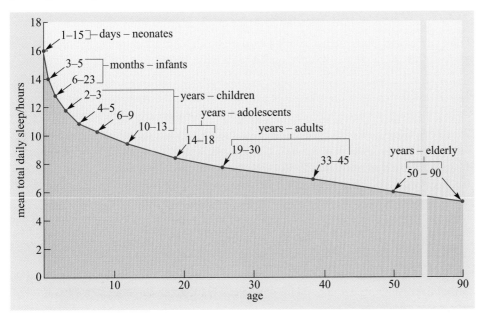

Figure 1.2 Changes with age in the total amounts of daily sleep.

◆ For the first example, explain why neither of the variables, amyloid plaques and cognitive impairment, is the independent variable.

◆ The independent variable is the one manipulated by the experimenter. In the case of amyloid plaques and cognitive impairment, neither variable is manipulated by an experimenter, so there is no independent variable.

Now because an independent variable has not been manipulated, it is not possible to make a causal inference; it is not possible to say a change in one variable effected a change in another variable. A correlation merely highlights a relationship; it may indicate a fruitful line of research but it does not allow a causal relationship to be inferred. It is salutary to consider the positive correlation between ice cream sales and drownings. It may be that ice cream consumption does impair swimming ability, but it may also be that a third variable has a positive effect on both ice cream sales and the number of people swimming in the sea.

A correlation does not imply causality.

The ability to infer causality is one main advantage of the experimental approach. Experiments involve manipulation and therefore can investigate causal inferences. Observational studies do not involve manipulation and they can reveal relationships, but not the causes of those relationships.

Summary of Sections 1.2.4 to 1.2.6

A procedure for eliminating experimenter bias or participant expectations is the blind trial. An experiment in which either the participants do not know to which condition they belong, or the experimenter does not know the condition to which the participant under observation belongs is a blind experiment. A double-blind experiment is one in which neither the participant nor the experimenter knows to which condition the participant belongs. A correlation highlights a relationship between two variables, but because neither variable has been manipulated by an experimenter, neither variable is an independent variable, and a causal inference cannot be made.

1.2.7 Measuring variables

There are a number of actions we take when we run an experiment that are so obvious that we do them without thinking. Whatever tasks we set or observations we make in our experiment, we end up with numbers. We need numbers because numbers can be easily compared. At the risk of being very boring, the next paragraph spells out what you do when you convert a variable into numbers.

We saw in Section 1.1.2 that a variable is something that can take different values. When you run an experiment, what you want to know is whether those values are different in each of your conditions. The only way you can know whether values are different is by using numbers. The process of using numbers to describe values is called **quantifying**, as opposed to using words to describe values, which is called *qualifying*. You quantify the values of your variable in each condition of your experiment. Just to round things off, you quantify values by *measuring* them, or by *counting* them. All this means is that you measure variables and generate numbers! These numbers, you will recall, are data.

In the following subsections, we look at aspects of measuring variables that are relevant to the study of behaviour.

Levels of measurement

It is important to distinguish between levels of measurement, because different statistical tests require different levels of measurement, and statistical tests are necessary to analyse your data. There are three relevant levels of measurement and these are **interval**, **ordinal** and **nominal** (or categorical).

(a) Interval level measurements. These are what you might think of as 'real' measurements, like height, reaction time, and so on. The distinguishing feature of this level of measurement is that you can assess the size of the differences between measurements. For example, if three participants had reaction times of 9, 13 and 11 seconds, then you can meaningfully say that the difference in reaction time between the first two (4 seconds) is larger than the difference between the last two (2 seconds).

(b) Ordinal level measurements. These are measurements where it is possible to say that one is larger than another, and so rank them with respect to each other, but it is impossible to assess the size of the differences. For example, you may be able to assess the extent of parental contact with their offspring using the following rating scale: (1) no contact; (2) hand contact; (3) holding around the chest; (4) cuddling.

It would be possible to assign any parental contact under investigation to one or other of four points on the scale. Hence you could rank contact in different experimental conditions (i.e. presence or absence of strangers) and say that contact at point 2 was less than contact at point 4. Here, though, it would not be meaningful to say that the difference between points 1 and 2 contact is any larger or smaller than the difference between points 3 and 4 contact. Hence, this is measurement at the ordinal level, because you can do no more than rank the measurements in order.

(c) Nominal (or categorical) level measurements. These are measurements where you can do no more than say that the variable measured belongs to this or that particular category. There is no sense in which you can arrange the categories in any order, such that one category ranks higher than another. For instance, people can be classified as being pedestrians or motorists; these two states do not have any order or rank and they are therefore nominal level measurements. In this respect categorical level measurements differ from ordinal ones. Typically, with nominal data, you simply count the number of items falling into each category.

At each level, the number of times a particular event occurs within a certain period or area is called its *frequency*. For example the frequency of pedestrians going down a road in five minutes might be 7 and the frequency of motorists might be 84.

In general, you should always think very carefully about what you are going to measure in an experiment. And you must be especially careful that you do not confuse the numbers themselves with *what the numbers actually mean.* For example, if, in an experiment, a participant rates the attractiveness of a set of photographs on a scale of 1 to 5, this may result in ratings of, say, 1, 3 and 5, for the three photographs. Now, according to the numbers themselves, the difference between 1 and 3 is the same as the difference between 3 and 5 (i.e. the *numbers* form an interval scale). But, *in terms of what the numbers actually mean* this is not really true. I cannot be sure that the difference between a rating of 1 and 3 *means* the same to the participant as the difference between 3 and 5. For example, the photos rated 1 and 3 might appear quite similar to the participant, while the final photo appears much more attractive. Thus *ratings* are often regarded as an ordinal scale, even though the numbers used to represent them have interval properties.

You have to be particularly careful about measurement scales when using statistics. Remember that statistical tests do not know what the numbers mean, they simply manipulate them to produce a result. But each statistical test is based upon some assumptions about the properties of the numbers that are fed into it (e.g. they must come from an interval scale). It is up to you, the experimenter, to make sure that these assumptions are valid. If they are not, the statistical test will still produce a result, but that result may well be meaningless. For example, if I count three number 4 buses and two number 18 buses, does it make sense to describe the mean bus number as 9.6?

Defining behaviour

In experiments it is extremely important to make it clear what aspects of behaviour you are recording. This should seem like an obvious condition of any experiment! After all, to record a cat as sleeping you have to know what a sleeping cat looks like. To record 'cuddling' you need to know what cuddling is, and so on. Superficially this does not seem like a problem. In this text so far we have used the examples of sleep, headaches and contact, without any need to define what these things are, so why do we now need a section devoted to defining behaviour?

The answer is simple. Behaviour is a minutely graded sequence of actions, as well as being a combination of actions, so there are many possible variations of the behaviour in question. Take a very simple example of measuring sleeping. Suppose the participant is yawning when you look at her – is she sleeping? Suppose the participant is stretching or adjusting her position – is she sleeping? You may think these are trivial points, and in truth the decision to include, for example, participants who are adjusting their position as asleep and yawning participants as awake, is arbitrary, but you need to know in order to make a record of that observation. In the example of parental contact, does hand contact mean hand of parent in contact with the child or hand of child in contact with the parent? It may not really matter exactly how you define the behaviour in question, there is no 'right answer', but you need to know and you need to be consistent. In defining the behaviour you are setting the criteria by which you will include observations in your records or exclude observations from your records.

Defining precisely the behaviour that you observe is not simply being pedantic; there is a very good reason for it. This is that, at a later date, someone else may wish to repeat your observations or experiments, perhaps because they do not believe them or because they wish to carry out further experiments based on yours. Repeatability of observations and experiments is a very important aspect of science and is the reason why scientists use standard units (seconds, millimetres, etc.) for making measurements. Only if you have described the behaviour that you have observed accurately and fully can another investigator repeat your experiment accurately. And, more generally, of course, the way in which you define your measures will ultimately determine what they mean and what can be learned from them.

Another aspect to this topic of defining behaviour is the distinction between *observing* behaviour and *interpreting* behaviour. A bird flying along with a twig in its beak may be nest building. It may also be performing a sexual display or even about to use the twig as a tool to catch ants. The observation that you can record is 'twig in beak'. Sometime later you may have more information and be in a position to interpret the behaviour as nest building or whatever. The observation is what you actually see. If you were interested in maternal behaviour in mice you would record suckling, licking or cleaning – all the activities you can see that happen when a mother interacts with her offspring. Later on it would be possible to interpret the observation 'suckling' as a *component* of maternal behaviour.

Experiments with more than one experimenter

In some experiments it is necessary to include a second experimenter. This is often the case in long-term studies or where long periods of uninterrupted observation are required. In this situation it is crucial that both experimenters are recording the same behaviour patterns, otherwise the data are meaningless. There is also no possibility of double checking (unless the behaviour patterns are all recorded on videotape), so it is important to establish consistency between experimenters, before the experiment starts.

Consistency between experimenters is achieved by having clearly defined behaviour and often by doing some simultaneous observations. If both experimenters record the behaviour of the same participants simultaneously then their records should be identical. Invariably such records show close, but not total, agreement. The degree of agreement between two experimenters is called *inter-experimenter reliability.* There are statistical methods of showing how good the inter-experimenter reliability is and whether it is good enough to allow their data to be combined.

Summary of Section 1.2.7

The actual value that a variable takes is obtained by counting or by measuring it; a process called quantifying. Quantifying variables produces numbers, or frequencies. Variables can be measured using interval, ordinal or nominal levels of measurement. The recorded behaviour patterns need to be carefully defined so it is clear whether to include or exclude a particular variation on the behaviour in question. Observed behaviour is behaviour that is actually seen. The behaviour may be subject to interpretation either by function or by grouping with other related behaviours. Where more than one experimenter is involved in an experiment some measure of inter-experimenter reliability must be obtained.

1.3 Experimental design

Although experiments have a universal basic structure, they vary in design and complexity. For instance, they may have one or more than one independent variable, any or all of which may be in a within- or a between-participants experimental design (see Sections 1.3.1 and 1.3.2). This guide concentrates on simple designs because they are simpler to execute and the results are easier to interpret. More complex designs are considered in other statistics texts. As a rule of thumb, always start with the simplest possible (often two condition) experiment, and then justify each refinement or complication you propose to add. Strive for simplicity and elegance. There is little point in designing a time-consuming experiment to investigate the role of several variables (e.g. gender, size, temperature) in determining some effect before you have established that the basic effect exists.

1.3.1 Experimental designs with one independent variable

Suppose you wanted to investigate the effects of an illegal, albeit frequently used, substance, such as MDMA (methylenedioxymethamphetamine or Ecstasy), on cognitive function. You know any effect is going to be subtle, because the cognitive function of people who have taken MDMA is not conspicuously different from that of people who have not taken it. To establish what, if any, effects there are, it would be necessary to conduct experiments.

There are lots of ways these experiments could be done. Some measure of cognitive function, for example a memory test of some sort, could be administered 24 hours after the participants took the MDMA. Immediately, it is obvious that a series of questions needs to be answered before the experiment begins: which measure(s) of cognitive function should be used, what time interval between drug administration and test administration should be used, where should the drug be administered, how much MDMA should be administered?

As you can see, there are numerous possible experimental designs; the exact one chosen depends on the answers to these questions. All the designs address the same issue, and they would all yield valid, if slightly different, conclusions. The designs vary in the decisions taken about the independent variable, the MDMA in this case (method of presentation, timing of presentation, what to present, i.e. pure MDMA, or MDMA mixed with some other substance(s) such as caffeine or ephedrine, as most illegally obtained MDMA is), and the dependent variable, cognitive function.

However, even after deciding on the precise question to examine, having chosen the independent variable and dependent variable, and having set the levels on the independent variable, there is one fundamental feature of the design that still needs a decision: how to distribute the participants across the conditions (how to allocate the participants to the various conditions).

Suppose the decision is made to administer the drug in a laboratory setting, and suppose the measure of cognitive performance is to be the number of words correctly recalled immediately after the presentation of a target list. Suppose also that there are a number of conditions based on dosage level (e.g. 75 mg, 100 mg, 125 mg). How are the participants to be distributed across the various conditions? An experiment with one experimental condition (one dosage level) and one control condition illustrates the two possibilities.

◆   Should anything be administered to the participants in the control condition?

◆   The participants in the control condition should be administered with something that looks, tastes and feels like the drug administered to the experimental participants, but which is known to be inactive (inert); that is, a placebo.

One possibility is that each participant should be tested in each condition – once with the MDMA and once with the inert substance. This is known as a **within-participants design**. It is called a within-participants design because when we compare the data from the different conditions, we are actually comparing data from the same participants. Hence our statistical comparisons are made *within* participants.

A second possibility is to test one group of participants with the MDMA and a different group of participants with the inert substance. Such a design – one in which *different* participants are used in each of the conditions – is known as a **between-participants design**. It is called a between-participants design because, when the data from the conditions are compared, the comparison is of data from different participants. Hence, statistical comparisons are made *between* participants.

These, then, are two basic designs: the between-participants design, in which a different batch of participants is used for each of the conditions in the experiment;

and the within-participants design, in which the same batch of participants is used throughout. In the between-participants design, the more conditions there are, the more participants are needed, because each condition requires its own batch of participants. This is not the case in the within-participants design, which means that within-participants designs need fewer participants. However, each participant needs to do more work.

The factors to bear in mind when deciding which design to use in your experiment are considered in the following subsection.

Summary of Section 1.3.1

Two basic experimental designs are the between-participants design and the within-participants design. In the between-participants design, a *different* set of participants is allocated to each condition. In the within-participants design, the *same* set of participants appears in every condition.

1.3.2   Choosing a within- or a between-participants design

In order to consider how you might choose between these designs, we must think back to the logic of experimental design discussed earlier. The aim is to manipulate the independent variable and examine what impact this manipulation has upon the dependent variable. If we find that there are indeed changes in the dependent variable, we may be able to infer that there is a causal link between them.

However, as we pointed out earlier, in order to make this causal inference we have to ensure that the independent variable really is the only thing that we are changing systematically in the situation, i.e. we do not want any confounding variables arising from our particular sample of participants. Thus, in the MDMA and cognitive function experiment, for example, there should not be many more users of other drugs, tobacco say, in the one condition rather than in the other. If there were, it may be that any differences observed in the dependent variable (e.g. number of items on the list correctly recalled) could be due to differences between smokers and non-smokers and not to basic differences in response to the experimental situation. Remember that confounding variables make the relationship between the dependent variable and the independent variable unclear, because they provide possible alternative explanations, e.g. that any difference in memory function in the two conditions is due to differences between smokers and non-smokers rather than to the consumption or non-consumption of MDMA. Essentially, the two types of design differ in the nature and extent of their potentially confounding variables. For example, suppose the MDMA experiment were run as a between-participants design, and it was found that those participants tested with the MDMA recalled fewer items on the list than those tested without the MDMA. This result could of course be because MDMA affects memory, but as was pointed out earlier, it could also be simply because more non-smokers were put into the control condition. There are pronounced individual differences in response to drugs and experimental situations. Any differences in response between groups of different participants, therefore, might well stem from this basic fact of life, rather than from any manipulation of the independent variable. In a between-participants design, of course, comparisons are made between the performances of different participants.

Now there are ways to minimize the impact of individual differences upon an experiment (Section 1.3.4), but there is only one way potentially to eliminate this source of extraneous variation. This is to use a within-participants design.

In a within-participants design the performances of different participants are not compared. Instead, the performances of the same participants on different occasions are compared. So, in the MDMA experiment each participant would be tested once with MDMA and once with the inert substance. It should then be safe to assume that any differences between their performance under the two conditions cannot stem from individual differences – because the same participants are tested in both conditions.

The within-participants design, therefore, avoids the problem of individual differences in ability to perform the experimental task. In formal terms, in eliminating individual differences from an experiment, the within-participants design reduces the amount of inherent, background or extraneous variation, i.e. variation other than that arising from the manipulation of the independent variable. For this reason within-participants designs are, at least in principle, to be preferred to between-participants ones.

As you have to start somewhere, therefore, a good rule of thumb when designing experiments is to start by exploring the possibility of using a within-participants design, and only turn to the alternatives when you discover obstacles that prevent the meaningful use of this design.

Summary of Section 1.3.2

In all experiments the effects of the independent variable on the dependent variable are assessed against a background of inherent or extraneous variation. Individual differences in ability to perform the experimental task are a considerable source of such extraneous variation. The within-participants design, in eliminating individual differences, removes a large part of this extraneous variation. It should, therefore be used in preference to the between-participants design when there are no insurmountable obstacles to its use.

1.3.3   Within-participants designs

The within-participants design is preferable in principle to the between-participants design. However, this does not mean that it is without problems and difficulties of its own.

Advantages

The major advantage of the within-participants design is that it reduces the background variation against which to assess the impact of the independent variable upon the dependent variable. It does this by eliminating the contaminating influence of individual differences. There is also a practical advantage that you will probably find extremely useful – you need fewer participants. Using fewer participants may also be preferable on ethical grounds if the experimental procedure involves any pain or distress to participants.

Disadvantages

If it eliminates one source of variation, the within-participants design unfortunately introduces another – **order effects**. When we run a within-participants design, by definition we will obtain more than one score from each participant. In which case, of course, we will have to present our conditions one after the other. The sequential presentation of conditions produces problems of its own, problems that do not exist with a between-participants experiment.

To return to the MDMA experiment, suppose it was run as a within-participants design, testing each participant first with the inert substance and then with the MDMA.

◆ If there was no effect, it could be that the MDMA had no effect. There is, however, an alternative explanation based on the order in which the participants experienced the two conditions. What is it?

◆ It could be that during the inert substance phase of the experiment the participants acquired a strategy for doing the memory test and that the strategy was effective when they were tested with the MDMA. Thus the *experience* of doing the test overrode the effect of the independent variable.

Order effects are the price paid for eliminating the influence of individual differences in a within-participants design. There are two forms of order effects: there are those that lead to an *improvement* in the participant's performance – things like practice, increasing familiarity with the experimental task and equipment or experience; and there are those that lead to a *deterioration* in their performance – things like loss of motivation due to fatigue or boredom. Both sorts of order effects need to be controlled.

1.3.4 Controlling order effects

The best way of controlling order effects is by employing a technique known as **counterbalancing**. This technique ensures that each condition in an experiment follows and is preceded by every other condition an equal number of times. Thus, for each participant who performs in one particular sequence of conditions, there are other participants who perform under all the other possible combinations of conditions. Although in the abstract this sounds complicated, generally it can be achieved comparatively easily. So, for instance, in the MDMA experiment, a very simple control for order effects would be to ensure that half of the participants were tested with the MDMA *before* they were tested with the inert substance, whilst the other half were tested with the MDMA *after* they had been tested with the inert substance (see Table 1.1). That way, although order effects would not have been eliminated (the experience of the test might well affect the participant's behaviour in the second condition) they would have been rendered *unsystematic*. That is, experience should affect the MDMA condition about as much as it affects the inert substance condition.

Table 1.1 Allocation of eight participants to order of testing.

Participant No.	Order in which participants encounter the two conditions	
	First condition	Second condition
1	inert substance	MDMA
2	MDMA	inert substance
3	inert substance	MDMA
4	MDMA	inert substance
5	inert substance	MDMA
6	MDMA	inert substance
7	inert substance	MDMA
8	MDMA	inert substance

In this example there are two conditions and only two orders or sequences in which the conditions can be presented – inert substance followed by MDMA, and MDMA followed by inert substance. If there were three conditions there would be six ($3 \times 2 \times 1$) orders; if there were five conditions there would be 120 ($5 \times 4 \times 3 \times 2 \times 1$) orders. A proper counterbalanced experiment with 120 orders would need a minimum of 120 participants (one for each order). This may be manageable, but sometimes there are too many conditions to counterbalance. Under these circumstances there is an alternative: to randomize the order of the conditions.

Randomization of the order of the conditions does not actually ensure that all the conditions are followed by and preceded by every other condition an equal number of times. Instead, it is a second best – a hope that a *random sequence* will spread the order effects more or less equally around the various conditions. For instance, if the orders in which the participants performed in an experiment with six experimental conditions were correctly randomized, each of the conditions should appear in each position (first, second, third, etc.) just about as often as the others. The more participants there are, the more likely it is that this will be the case. If there are several tasks to perform in each condition then the order of tasks should also be randomized.

This is because the critical feature of a random sequence is that the items in the sequence all have an equal chance of being selected for any of the positions in that sequence. In the case of orders, what this means is that any of the conditions can appear first, second, third, etc., for any of the participants. So, for example, in an experiment with six conditions A–F, condition A has the same chance as conditions B, C, D, E and F, of being the first condition undertaken by participant 1. If condition C is the one actually chosen (see Section 1.4.2 for the details of how to go about making such choices), then conditions A, B, D, E and F, all have an equal chance of being the second condition undertaken by participant 1. If condition D is chosen as the second condition, then conditions A, B, E and F, all have an equal chance of being the third condition undertaken by participant 1, and so on until all the conditions have been allocated to this participant. Moreover, the same applies to participant 2, and indeed to *all* the participants in the experiment (Table 1.2).

Table 1.2 Randomized orders of conditions for eight participants in a within-participants design experiment with four conditions. Each order has been created randomly and separately for each participant. The letters A, B, C and D refer to the four different conditions.

Participant No.	Order			
	1	2	3	4
1	C	D	A	B
2	B	D	A	C
3	D	B	A	C
4	A	C	B	D
5	A	D	B	C
6	A	B	C	D
7	D	B	A	C
8	C	D	B	A

It is worth taking a close look at what is meant by an order effect. Consider the first participant in Table 1.2, and suppose the task was to stack as many blocks as possible in two minutes – each condition being a different colour of block. C = red, D = green, A = yellow, B = blue. Clearly, by the time the first participant gets to the yellow and blue blocks (conditions A and B) he or she is likely to be tired. So the first participant's data are of no use on their own – they are confounded by the order effect of fatigue. Only the *overall* data can be analysed, because only when all the participants' data are pooled are the systematic effects of fatigue eliminated. In this example, the nature of each condition does not really matter – it is a reasonable assumption that stacking yellow blocks is just as tiring, boring and easy as stacking red blocks. However, suppose conditions A–D represented different doses of MDMA, and one of these doses (D) made the participant ill. The effect of this illness might be present in the next condition, condition A for this first participant.

Where one condition actually affects another, there is said to be a **carry-over effect**. Now carry-over effects cannot be eliminated, but randomizing or counterbalancing the order can prevent a carry-over effect from *systematically* affecting the data. (Notice that in Table 1.2 only for participants 1 and 2 does condition A immediately follow condition D.) If the carry-over effect is only temporary, then its impact could be reduced by introducing a longer than usual time-delay between conditions (e.g. days, or even weeks). However, if this strategy is not feasible (e.g. lack of time, lack of cooperation on the part of your participants), or if the effect is more durable, then it would be wise to employ one of the alternative designs (e.g. the between-participants design). For example, if we were attempting to compare two different techniques of teaching a particular task, once the participants have learned the task, it is basically impossible to make them unlearn it in order to learn it once again by the different method. Similarly, in much drug research, it is difficult to have a no-drug condition following immediately upon a drug condition. So you must watch out for treatment conditions in your experiments that tend to alter markedly the state of your participant, and consider ways of dealing with these carry-over effects.

Summary of Section 1.3.4

The cost of eliminating the confounding influences of individual differences in the within-participants design is the introduction of another source of extraneous variation-order effects. Order effects are of two kinds: those that lead to an improvement and those that lead to a deterioration in performance of the experimental task. Two methods are used to control these order effects: counterbalancing and randomizing the order of the conditions. These methods do not eliminate the variation introduced by order effects. They simply transform it into unsystematic variation. Where one condition affects another there is a carry-over effect. Under these circumstances the use of between-participants designs must be seriously considered.

1.3.5 Between-participants designs

Where there are insurmountable order effects, or when the participants simply have to be different (e.g. in learning experiments or in tests that investigate differences between species, strain or the sexes) then the within-participants design is not suitable. Under these circumstances, you should turn to the alternative: the between-participants design. More complex designs (e.g. mixed designs with more than one independent variable in which some independent variables are within and others are between participants) are possible, but are not considered here.

With only one independent variable, the alternative to the within-participants design is the between-participants design. The advantage of the between-participants design corresponds to the weakness of the within-participants design. That is, there are no problems with order effects. Clearly, the biggest disadvantage of the between-participants design is the presence of individual differences, but there are ways to minimize their impact on the experiment.

As always, the objective of controlling for any individual differences is to rule out any systematic effects stemming from such differences between participants. Although it is not possible to eliminate individual differences, it is possible to try to distribute them equally across conditions, e.g. to try to allocate as many smokers to the MDMA condition as to the inert substance condition. Random allocation of participants to conditions might achieve this, especially if there is a large number of participants. (This topic is covered in Section 1.4.2.)

An alternative, however, where you can recognize relevant features, is to match the participants; this is the matched-participants design. **Matching** means grouping like with like and ensuring that an equal number of each group (matched set) is in each condition. In the present example, matching might mean assessing smoking and then making sure that equal numbers of smokers and non-smokers were allocated to each condition. In order to do this, it would obviously be necessary to assess the participants *prior* to running the experiment.

Matching then requires the establishment of different groups of participants, such that within any one group participants are of equal or similar ability (or status or size or whatever). The next stage is to allocate the matched participants to the experimental conditions randomly. That is, you must decide which particular condition any one of the smokers or any one of the non-smokers is to go in, at random, in exactly the same way that you would do with a sample of non-matched participants.

◆   Why is the random allocation of matched participants to conditions necessary?

◆   With the non-random allocation of participants to conditions there is the possibility of a confounding variable arising, just as with non-matched participants.

This is a real problem when animals for testing are kept in groups. There is a tendency for the experimenter to select animals that are easiest to handle, and thus inadvertently select placid animals in preference to non-placid ones. In this way placid animals could constitute the participants for condition A and non-placid animals could constitute the participants for condition B. A confounding variable of this sort can be eliminated by prior allocation of the animals to the conditions. This is covered in Section 1.4.2.

Matched participants, therefore, still need to be allocated to experimental conditions randomly. This is done by turning to each group of matched participants separately. So, for instance, you might start with your matched group of smokers and allocate them to their conditions using the methods described in Section 1.4.2. Once all these had been allocated to their conditions (ensuring an equal number of them appears in each condition) you might then turn to the non-smokers and repeat the process. In this way there would be a spread of smokers and non-smokers in each condition.

Although matching is a useful technique, it does have limitations. People and animals vary in many different ways, so it is not usually possible to match all their characteristics. The experimenter often has to decide beforehand which characteristics are most relevant to the experiment and thus which should be matched. One common trick is to perform a pre-test of all participants on the relevant dependent variable. Here, for example, we could administer a preliminary memory test. We can then match participants according to their scores on the preliminary test and thus ensure that each group contains participants of similar ability.

Summary of Section 1.3.5

The between-participants design eliminates order effects. However, in doing so, it introduces individual differences and requires larger numbers of participants than the equivalent within-participants design. Individual differences may be controlled for by allocating the participants to conditions randomly. This does not eliminate the variation introduced by individual differences; it is simply an attempt to render them unsystematic. As with controlling for order effects by randomization, it is possible that allocating participants randomly to conditions does not completely transform the systematic variation. This should be borne in mind when findings are interpreted.

A good half-way house between the within-participants and between-participants design is to use a between-participants design in which the participants have been matched and allocated to conditions such that there is an equal spread of ability on the experimental task between the conditions. This is known as the matched-participants design, and it reduces the possibility of individual differences confounding the effects of the independent variable.

1.4   Participants

1.4.1   Choosing participants

It is axiomatic that every individual is unique. Yet the objective of any experiment is to be able to make general statements about classes or groups of individuals. There is no way of completely resolving this conflict between individual characteristics and common performance. The best that can be done is to try to reduce the amount of variation between the participants in an experiment. To minimize individual variation, differences between identifiable groups of individuals are acknowledged and participants selected from within a particular group. For example, adults would be acknowledged to be a different group from children; drug addicts a different group from non-addicts; Open University students a different group from conventional undergraduates, and so on. Each additional factor or criterion used to identify a member of a group reduces the variation of the group. So for example, if the criteria for inclusion in a group are mature, female undergraduates or boys whose fathers are alcoholics, then the variation between the individuals included within those groups is considerably narrowed compared to the broad group, people. Whatever criteria are used, however a particular group of participants is defined, the entire membership of that group is the **population** and any results become applicable only to that population.

In the malted beverage and sleep experiment you might choose the population 'normal healthy adults with sleep problems', or 'normal healthy adults who feel tired during the day'. Now it would be impossible to do an experiment in which you had to test all normal healthy adults who feel tired during the day; there are too many of them! So what is needed is a representative group of them, a **sample** of normal healthy adults who feel tired during the day, on which to do the experiment. A sample of, say, 20 normal healthy adults who feel tired during the day would, it is hoped, be representative of the population of normal healthy adults who feel tired during the day.

The term sample means a representative part. In a statistical context, a sample is a group of participants, or measurements, taken from a population and representative of that population.

Once the population has been defined, the next task is to select the sample. First, what is an appropriate size for the sample? How big should it be? There is no correct answer to this question, but there are two opposing constraints.

Small samples (less than 20 participants)   Small samples are easy to manage and obtain, and do not take long to test. However, small samples are very sensitive to individual differences; one aberrant individual can drastically alter the overall result. A small sample might be overloaded with geniuses for the particular task, for instance, and so distort the results. This distortion means that even if an effect exists, even if the independent variable does influence the dependent variable, the effect is unlikely to be found. The smaller the sample, the less representative it is of the whole population.

Large samples (more than 20 participants)   Large samples are more difficult to find and manage, and may take a long time and be costly to test. A large number of participants is likely to include a range of abilities, i.e. those who are good, bad and indifferent at doing the experimental task. Furthermore, the more participants there are to test, the more likely it is that any eccentric performance by particular individuals will be mirrored by eccentric performances by other individuals in the opposite direction and so be cancelled out. With large samples, the performances of a few aberrant individuals will be masked by the mass. With large samples, if an effect exists, if the independent variable does influence the dependent variable, it is likely to be found. A large number of participants is more likely to be representative of the whole population.

A second issue that needs to be considered is the size of the effect – the degree to which the independent variable influences the participants. If the size of the effect is large, then it will be revealed even with relatively few participants. If the size of the effect is small, then the effect may only be revealed with a large number of participants. The relationship between the size of the sample and the size of the effect arises because, with a small effect, the performance of many of the participants in the experimental group will be very similar to the performance of many of the participants in the control group. Only by using a large number of participants will the small effect be revealed. This relationship is considered again in Section 1.5.

A rule of thumb is to use as many participants as can be managed, with a minimum in each condition determined by the statistical test that will be used to analyse the data (see Section 1.5).

Having determined the size of the sample, the next task is actually to select it. The sample must be representative of the population. Thus the population must be defined and then effective criteria for determining membership of that population must be determined.

The decisions taken about the definition of the population and the criteria for selection determine effectively how representative the results will be. If the experiment is about addiction but the sample is chosen only from alcoholics, then you cannot say whether the results apply to all addicts, or merely to those addicted to alcohol. The definition of the population and the selection criteria depend crucially on the statement you want to make at the end of the study.

Once you have a sample it is necessary to brief potential participants and then to allocate actual participants to the various conditions. The next two sections address the issues of briefing potential participants and allocating them to conditions.

1.4.2 Informed consent

You need to inform all potential participants of the objectives of the investigation. You also need to inform the potential participants of all aspects of the research or intervention that might reasonably be expected to influence their willingness to participate. You will have already considered the safety of the experiment and ensured that the experiment is safe and does not expose the participants to harm, either physical or mental. During the briefing, the potential participants have the opportunity to make their own judgement about risk, and to withdraw from your pool of potential participants whenever they wish. In addition, you should explain all other aspects of the research or intervention about which the potential participants may enquire. After being briefed about the experiment, potential participants should be asked to give their written consent: this is the principle of **informed consent**. Only those potential participants who give their consent become participants. Participants may withdraw from the experiment at any time.

If you wish to read more about informed consent, see *Ethical Principles for conducting Research with Human Participants*, published by the British Psychological Society. This is available on the Society's website at http://www.bps.org.uk/the-society/the-society_home.cfm [accessed September 2005].

1.4.3 Randomizing

Randomizing is an essential skill of experimental work – one that is consistently underrated by both teachers and students. The whole strength of the experiment as a tool for enabling us to make causal inferences depends in many ways on our ability to allocate randomly participants to conditions or conditions to participants. Fail to do this and one of the basic controls for confounding variables is lost.

You have already encountered a number of situations where randomization is needed.

◆ Describe two of the situations where randomization is needed.

◆ The first is when you need to randomize the order in which you present the conditions to your participants (e.g. in a within-participants design). The second is the technique that is most generally employed to control for the effects of individual differences in a between-participants design – the random allocation of participants to conditions.

What follows is a description of the basic technique of randomization. It is important to realize, however, that the fundamental principle of randomization is that for whatever you are randomizing – be it orders or participants or conditions – any given item should have an equal chance of selection at all times. Thus the prior selection of one particular item (e.g. low dosage condition) should not affect in any way the chances of any of the other items (low, medium or high dosage condition) being subsequently selected. So, for example, in selecting orders for participants, the chances of any given order being selected, e.g. the order B A C, must not be affected by any selections that you have made previously, e.g. the order C A B. Similarly, when allocating participants to conditions, the chances of a given participant appearing in one particular condition should not be affected by previous allocations of participants to that or any other condition.

What this means in practice is that we do not simply sit down and juggle orders around or allocate participants to conditions in what seems to be a suitably random order. Neither do we generate numbers from our heads. Such methods do not yield truly random results because people will inevitably tend to reject obviously structured sequences (e.g. 1, 2, 3, 4, 5, 6) which do not appear to be random. Yet randomization requires that such a sequence should be just as likely as any other. Instead, randomizing tools are used – devices that enable the generation of truly random sequences and whose results we obey, however non-random they might occasionally appear.

Now, all that is required of these tools is that they determine choices in an unbiased way, i.e. that they do not favour some outcomes more than others. Consequently, if used properly, items such as coins, playing cards and dice are perfectly adequate for this purpose. In addition, most textbooks of statistics include tables of random numbers. (Appendix 1.1 contains an example of part of a random number table.) These tables have been produced by a computer program that enabled the digits 0 to 9 to have an equal opportunity of appearing at any given position in the table. So, at any given position, there is no way of knowing which of these digits is likely to appear. Even if the previous twelve digits have all been '7' (which is extremely unlikely, but still possible) the chances of '7' appearing as the thirteenth digit are *exactly* the same as if there had been no '7' among the previous twelve. You can see, therefore, that such tables are ideally suited for the purposes of randomizing.

The digits in a random number table can be used singly, in pairs, in groups of three and so on. The important thing is not to keep entering the tables at the same place. If you do enter at the same place then you will simply be using the same sequence of numbers and your lists will not differ.

Finally, before trying some examples of randomizing, remember that randomizing is one of the things to be done, whenever possible, prior to running your experiments. That is, it is one of the elements of experimenting that should usually be organized in advance.

Using random number tables

Here is one procedure. Enter the table in Appendix 1.1 anywhere. Spin a coin to decide whether to proceed diagonally (heads) or along lines (tails). If tails, spin a coin to decide whether to move horizontally (heads) or vertically (tails). Then spin a coin to decide whether to move up or down (if moving vertically) or left or right (if moving horizontally). Proceed similarly if the original spin returned a head. This procedure is standard for the use of random number tables.

Allocating participants to conditions: between-participants designs

Suppose there are 18 participants to allocate to two conditions, condition A and condition B. Number the participants 1 to 18. Enter the table and proceed as directed above. Step through the table reading pairs of digits; odd numbers will represent condition A and even numbers will represent condition B. The order in which you come across these numbers in the table will dictate the order in which to allocate participants to conditions. For instance, consider the following sequence of random numbers:

   33 44 12 01 70 03 49 90 17 21 etc.

The first number, 33, is odd, so participant number 1 is allocated to condition A. The second number, 44, is even, so participant number 2 is allocated to condition B, and so on. It is necessary to ensure that an equal number of participants are allocated to each condition. Thus, as soon as half the participants have been allocated to one condition, any remaining participants must be allocated to the second condition. The final product will be a table like Table 1.3.

Table 1.3   Allocation of participants to conditions.

Participant No.	Condition	Participant No.	Condition
1	A	10	A
2	B	11	B
3	B	12	B
4	A	13	B
5	B	14	B
6	A	15	A
7	A	16	A
8	B	17	A
9	A	18	B

The next phase is to determine the order in which to test the participants.

Enter the table again, at a different place, and proceed as before. This time, though, the numbers are the numbers of the participants.

Consider the sequence:

18 15 61 87 92 05 12 15 22 90 98 19 62 01 29 18 30 15 07

The first number is 18, so participant 18 is tested first. The second number is 15, so participant 15 is tested second. The third number is 61, and as there is no participant 61 it is ignored. Similarly the fourth and fifth numbers are ignored.

Use the sequence of numbers above to determine which participant will be tested sixth.

Participant number 7 will be tested sixth. In the sequence only those numbers shown below in bold type are used, other numbers, including any repeats of particular numbers, are ignored.

Random number (i.e. participant number) = RN:

RN	**18**	**15**	61	87	92	**05**	**12**	15	22	90	98	19	62	**01**	29	18	30	15	**07**
Order	1	2				3	4							5					6

Obviously, this technique can be extended to more than two conditions.

Allocating orders to participants: within-participants designs

Even with a counterbalanced design you should allocate the orders to subjects randomly. For example, suppose there are six orders (three conditions) and twelve participants. Enter the table and proceed as directed above. Number the participants 1 to 12. Step through the table looking for pairs of digits, allocating the participants to the orders in sequence. For example, with the following line:

25 53 **04 01** 63 **08** 45 93 **12** 22

participant 4 would do order 1, participant 1 would do order 2, participant 8 would do order 3, and so on until all twelve participants had received an order. Again, you should disregard repeats of particular numbers.

1.4.3 The final stage

So far the whole procedure of experimental design has been a thought process, a mental exercise to determine the number of participants, which conditions to test them in, what order to test them, and so on. Underlying all of this thinking are the assumptions you have made about how the participants will behave in the experimental set-up: will the participants actually sleep, get headaches, or remember anything? There is only one way to find out whether your assumptions are valid and that is to try it and see, to test a few participants in accordance with the experimental schedule and see how they respond. You may find that the way you intended to handle your participants is entirely inappropriate, or that your participants are disturbed by the noise in the room, or that they misunderstand your instructions. By trying it out you are able to modify the experimental procedure before too many participants have been used. There is no substitute for this practical test. Often you will have spent a good deal of time trying to identify all the possible problems by thinking about the experiment – only to find that a quick run through of the procedure reveals an obvious, but unforeseen, difficulty.

Summary of Section 1.4

In choosing participants it is necessary to decide how far to restrict the group (population) from which to select them (sample). Deciding how many participants to select (i.e. the sample size) is a balance between the advantages of large numbers and the constraints of time, cost and other resources that large numbers impose. Randomizing the allocation of participants to conditions or the order in which the participants encounter the conditions is an essential part of experimental design. Randomization requires the use of random number tables or a random number generator of some sort. Prior to actually running an experiment it is essential that a small trial be run first, to ensure the proposed protocol actually works.

1.5   Using statistics

Statistics were introduced in Section 1.1.3. Averages, you will recall, are summary statistics and because they allow the data to be explored, they are sometimes called exploratory statistics. Such statistics may reveal patterns and they may suggest that participants in one condition performed better (or worse) than participants in the other condition. To test whether that is the case, confirmatory statistics are required. These confirmatory statistics are better known as statistical tests.

1.5.1   Beyond reasonable doubt: probability and statistics

So far this chapter has mentioned differences between conditions and correlations between variables. Now it is not just a question of there being a difference in participants' scores between, say, two conditions; what we are interested in are those differences or correlations that are reliable. Reliable differences are those that are likely to occur again if the experiment is repeated.

Anyone who plays or watches sport will know that an individual's performance varies day by day. Similarly, in an experiment, the performance of participants varies each time they perform the experimental task. And this change in performance occurs irrespective of any change in the independent variable. It has also been pointed out that there are profound individual differences between participants in their basic abilities on experimental tasks. Differences in performance of the same participant at different times and also between participants mean that, even where participants are allocated to conditions randomly, and tested in the *absence* of the independent variable, it would be unreasonable to expect exactly the same scores on the dependent variable by the participants in each condition. What this means in practice is that the scores of participants in condition A are going to be different from the scores of participants in condition B irrespective of any effect of the independent variable. Your duration of sleep for example, is probably different from one night to the next. This random or *chance* fluctuation in performance goes on continuously. Now think about the effect of drinking a malted beverage at bedtime on sleep duration. You need to distinguish any difference in the duration of your sleep that was due to the malted beverage, from any difference in the duration of your sleep that was due to chance fluctuation. It is always necessary to assess the effects of the independent variable against a background of inherent variation in performance of the dependent variable. This is the 'doubt' in the title to this chapter: that maybe the independent variable had no effect and the results of the experiment are just chance fluctuation? To get beyond that doubt, to prove a relationship between two events, the effect of the independent variable on the dependent variable has to be over and above chance fluctuation; the effect of the independent variable has to be shown to be unlikely to be due to chance fluctuation.

The need, therefore, is to find a way of being able to distinguish a difference that has been influenced by the independent variable, a **reliable** difference, from one that has not been so influenced, a difference that would be there anyway, chance variation. This is where inferential statistics come in.

Inferential statistics

This text does not go into any mathematics. There is no need to understand the mathematics behind any particular statistical test, just as there is no need to understand how a word processor works, so long as you can use it appropriately. However, it is helpful to be able to visualize what the statistical tests are doing, and that is the purpose of this section. A useful starting point is the normal distribution.

Two thousand and one hundred adults were asked how many hours they slept each night. The results are shown in Figure 1.3. The variable measured (sleep duration) is plotted on the horizontal axis. The number of people stating a particular sleep duration, or, put another way, the frequency with which a particular sleep duration was stated, is plotted on the vertical axis. The resulting graph is a *frequency distribution*.

The graph shows clearly what you might have predicted; most people sleep between seven and eight hours each night; very few people sleep for less than four

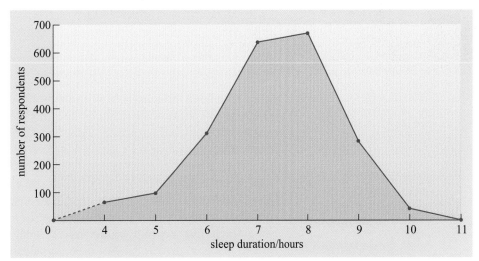

Figure 1.3 Daily sleep duration in hours, as reported by a sample of 2100 people.

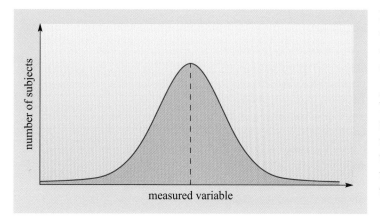

Figure 1.4   The classic normal distribution showing the line of symmetry at the mean value.

hours or more than ten hours each night. The shape of this graph, with few observations at either extreme and the bulk of observations in the middle, is characteristic of a *normal distribution*.

A classic normal distribution is shown in Figure 1.4. Note in particular that it is symmetrical about a midpoint along the horizontal axis. This midpoint is the mean. The vertical dashed line on the graph is at the midpoint, and the left-hand side of the graph is the mirror image of the right-hand side of the graph; the graph is symmetrical (Figure 1.4).

The normal distribution can be used in two main ways. Firstly, it can be used to identify and define observed values that are extreme or abnormal.

◆ Which mathematical way of describing the spread of values should be used in conjunction with the mean?

◆ The standard deviation (Section 1.1.3).

In a normal distribution, 95% of the observed values lie within 1.96 standard deviations on either side of the mean. (For simplicity, 1.96 is usually rounded up to 2.) Put another way, this means that only 5% of the observed values are more than two standard deviations above or below the mean.

◆ Why has the phrase 'above or below' been included in the previous sentence?

◆ Because the normal distribution is symmetrical, extreme values can be higher or lower than the mean.

◆ What percentage of observed values are two standard deviations below the mean?

◆ There are 2.5% of observed values two standard deviations below the mean. Likewise there are 2.5% of observed values two standard deviations above the mean.

Any value that is above or below the mean by more than two standard deviations is, by convention, defined as being abnormal.

The second and more usual way in which the normal distribution is used, is to compare data from two conditions. It is this comparison that is at the heart of a number of statistical tests, often referred to as *parametric* tests. Imagine three experiments, experiments 1, 2 and 3, each consisting of two conditions A and B, in which reaction time is measured in 2000 participants. The results from each experiment are plotted in Figures 1.5a, b and c. In experiment 1 the data from participants in condition B virtually match those from condition A; the frequency distributions almost totally overlap (Figure 1.5a). It is obvious that there is virtually no difference between the conditions; the independent variable had no obvious effect. In experiment 2, the data from participants in condition B are totally different from those of participants in condition A; the frequency distributions do not overlap at all (Figure 1.5b). Clearly, there is a difference between the conditions; the independent variable had a very marked (large) effect on the performance of participants in condition B. Whilst results do occasionally fit the pattern shown in experiments 1 and 2, the most usual pattern is that depicted by experiment 3. In experiment 3 there is overlap between the data from the two conditions (Figure 1.5c). Condition B data appear to have a slightly higher mean, but the effect of the independent variable on the performance of the participants is small. The question is, are the data from the two conditions really different? This question is a reformulation of an earlier question about finding a way of being able to recognize a difference that has been influenced by the independent variable – a reliable difference – from one that has not been so influenced, a difference that would be there anyway – chance variation.

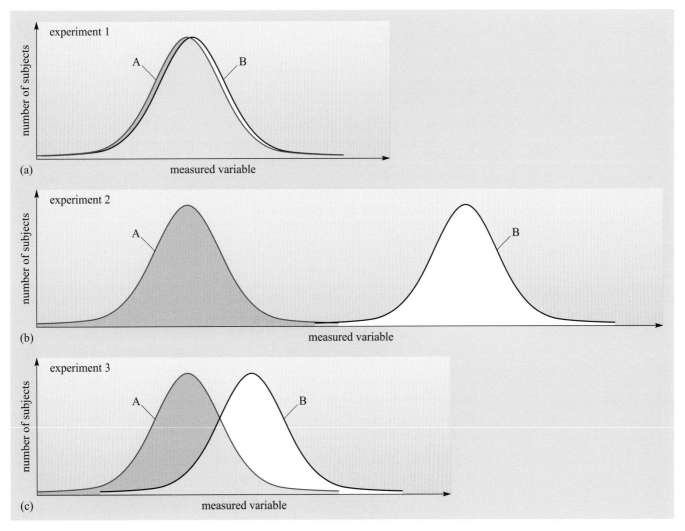

Figure 1.5 Hypothetical results from experiments 1, 2 and 3, each with two conditions A and B, plotted as frequency distributions: (a) experiment 1 showing distributions with virtually complete overlap of data; (b) experiment 2 showing distributions with virtually no overlap of data; (c) experiment 3 showing distributions with some overlap of data.

Now that you can visualize the problem in terms of distinguishing between results due to chance variation and those due to a real effect of the independent variable, we can move on to the more usual situation in experiments, where the sample is not thousands, but tens of participants. In this situation there are relatively few data points; and it simply is not possible to plot a meaningful frequency distribution. This does not matter: the earlier discussion of frequency distributions was to illustrate the concept. As long as it is sensible to calculate a mean and a standard deviation then that defines what the frequency distribution would look like, were you to plot it, and is also sufficient for statistical purposes.

Consider the data in Table 1.4, derived from an experiment in which positive air pressure was used to affect the duration of deep sleep. (You are not expected to concern yourself with details of the experiment from which the data were derived.)

There are two conditions, C1 in which treatment was not given, and C2 in which treatment was given.

◆ Which is the control, and which the experimental condition?

◆ C1 is the control condition and C2 is the experimental condition.

Notice that some participants in condition C1 spent longer in deep sleep than many participants in condition C2. Participant 22 (C1) spent longer in deep sleep than participants 1, 2, 3, 4, 5, 6, 7 and 8 (C2) for instance. Note too, that the shortest period of deep sleep in the two conditions was very similar: 1.8 minutes versus 1.9 minutes. Also, it is clear that more participants in C2 spent longer in deep sleep. Only six participants in C1 exceeded ten minutes of deep sleep, compared with 19 participants in C2. These descriptions of the data tell us firstly that the data from the two conditions overlap and secondly that a statistical test is required to determine whether the two sets of data are reliably different.

This is the question to be answered: is there a *reliable* difference between the two conditions? The null hypothesis for this experiment would be that there is no real difference in deep sleep duration that can be attributed to positive airway pressure. In other words, the null hypothesis states that the overall range of deep sleep duration across the two conditions, i.e. any variations between the two sets of data, could have arisen by chance. What is needed is a way of assessing how likely it is that the results in Table 1.4 arose by chance, i.e. this requires a statistical test. The statistical test is a mathematical way of calculating precisely how likely it is that a particular result arose by chance; the statistical test calculates the **probability** of a particular outcome.

Two general points are worth remembering. First, statistics do not produce definite answers; they deal with *probability* rather than certainty. Indeed, you will never know whether a particular set of results actually arose by chance or not; you will only know the probability that they arose by chance. Second, statistical logic asks how likely it is that the results arose by chance, or, more perversely, how unlikely it is that there is no effect of the independent variable. In other words, statistical inference is based on the null hypothesis, not the experimental hypothesis. Specifically, this kind of statistical testing works out the likelihood of your result if the null hypothesis is true (i.e. if there is no effect). We then simply define reliable effects as those that are sufficiently unlikely if the null hypothesis is true.

Table 1.4 Duration of deep* sleep (in minutes) in participants with breathing difficulties**; 27 without (C1) and 27 with (C2) continuous positive airway pressure treatment. Participants in each condition have been ranked by duration of deep sleep.

Participant rank	Condition C1 deep sleep/min	Participant rank	Condition C2 deep sleep/min
1	1.8	1	1.9
2	1.9	2	3.1
3	2.1	3	3.6
4	2.2	4	4.7
5	2.4	5	5.2
6	2.4	6	5.9
7	2.6	7	6.4
8	2.6	8	9.8
9	2.6	9	11.3
10	3.2	10	11.4
11	3.3	11	11.9
12	3.5	12	12.5
13	3.8	13	16.4
14	4.0	14	16.5
15	4.1	15	16.8
16	5.1	16	17.7
17	5.7	17	19.4
18	6.1	18	24.6
19	8.9	19	28.4
20	9.1	20	41.1
21	9.2	21	43.7
22	10.3	22	46.4
23	10.6	23	52.9
24	12.1	24	73.2
25	13.3	25	125.0
26	42.5	26	158.2
27	59.6	27	174.3

*Deep sleep was measured physiologically using a polysomnograph and was reported as stage 3/4 sleep.

**Participants were diagnosed with sleep apnea-hypopnea syndrome.

Consider the sleep experiment: 'Does a bedtime malted beverage affect the duration of sleep?' Now, to think about what the statistics are going to do, suppose the beverage has *no* effect.

◆ What kind of result would you expect?

◆ You would expect the results under the two conditions to be very similar.

If the actual data in the two conditions are similar, i.e. the results could well have arisen by chance, then the null hypothesis is accepted. If the actual data in the two conditions are dissimilar (i.e. the result probably did not arise by chance) then you reject the null hypothesis. You infer how similar or dissimilar the results from the conditions are by calculating the probability that the results arose by chance. That sentence is statistics in a nutshell.

Probabilities are usually expressed as p values, which give the probability that the data put into the statistical test arose by chance. A p value of 1 means that it is an absolute certainty that the results arose by chance; a p value of 0 means that it is impossible that the results arose by chance. In practice, p values of one or zero are very rare, but the nearer the p value is to zero, the more content the experimenter. This is because the smaller the p value is, the less likely the results are to have arisen by chance; the more likely there is a real difference between the conditions. For example if $p = 0.001$, then there is only a one in one thousand probability that the results arose by chance. Such a result would mean the null hypothesis could be rejected, leaving the experimental hypothesis to explain the data. It is customary to say that p has to be 0.05 or less before the null hypothesis can be rejected. (When $p = 0.05$, there is a one in twenty probability that the results arose by chance. Put another way, when $p = 0.05$, the probability is 19 to 1 against the results having arisen by chance.) With p less than 0.05 (usually written as $p < 0.05$) the result is said to be **statistically reliable** (or statistically significant), and the null hypothesis can be rejected. You may wonder why a p value of 0.05 was chosen as the threshold between reliability and non-reliability, rather than 0.04 or 0.01 or some other figure. There is no mathematical or logical reason why 0.05 was chosen, and indeed some experimenters prefer the value of 0.01. Historically though it is $p < 0.05$ which has come to be accepted as a reasonable threshold level of reliability, at which the null hypothesis can be rejected. Actual levels of probability are usually quoted in research papers, allowing the reader to apply their own level of reliability in evaluating the results.

In Section 1.2.2, the directional and bi-directional hypotheses were considered. One consequence of choosing a directional hypothesis is that the same data appear to be more reliable when tested. The mathematics dictate that data tested under a directional hypothesis can be statistically reliable, whereas the same data tested under a bi-directional hypothesis are not statistically reliable. This is the payoff for using a directional, or one-tailed hypothesis.

◆ What was the disadvantage of using the directional hypothesis?

◆ The disadvantage of using the directional hypothesis is that any difference in the data in the opposite direction to that predicted will be masked by the null hypothesis, which states that there is no difference. Such differences, however large, must be ignored.

1.5.2   Choosing a statistical test

There are statistical tests for all occasions and all types of data. Choosing the correct test for the particular occasion and a specific type of data requires a reasonable knowledge of statistical tests and what distinguishes one from another. The distinctions and procedures to use when choosing tests are beyond the scope of this course, but are covered in most books on statistics.

1.5.3   Power

Power is another statistical measure. Power is a measure of the ability to detect a reliable effect of the independent variable on the dependent variable, where such an effect exists. The details of which factors influence power and how power can be calculated need not concern you. However, you should note that the higher the power, on a scale of 0 to +1, the more likely it is that a real effect will be detected. So, for example, a large sample size increases the power, as does a large effect.

1.5.4   The numbers game

One final thing to remember about your analyses is that statistical procedures only deal with the numbers fed into them and they do not know the meaning of the numbers (Section 1.2.7). A statistical test will churn around any set of numbers fed in using a suitable format. The delivery of a statistic at the end of this process does not sanctify the data. Just because the data were analysed does not mean that either the analysis itself or its outcome was necessarily meaningful. Also, bear in mind that rejecting the null hypothesis does not automatically mean that the results went in the direction you predicted. It is worthwhile to look at the data once they have been analysed and to think about what the results mean. Get into the habit of going back to your data and thinking about what the outcome of your analyses might mean in terms of the question your experiment set out to answer.

Summary of Section 1.5

The data obtained from participants in one condition of an experiment are usually not completely different from those obtained from participants in another condition: the data are said to overlap. Provided it is sensible to calculate a mean and standard deviation, then it is possible to carry out some mathematics to establish the probability that the data from the two conditions came from the same population. The mathematics is a statistical test, and if the calculated probability is small, then the data probably came from two different populations; a reliable difference has been established. The low probability also means that the null hypothesis can be rejected. At this point the data should be re-examined to establish what they mean in the context of the experiment.

1.6 Student's *t*-test

You are required to perform only one statistical test in this course and that is the Student's *t*-test. The Student's *t*-test is a robust, well-documented test that compares the means of two sets of data. The end result of the test is a single value of '*t*' which is a measure of the extent to which the two sets of data overlap. Remember, where the data extensively overlap, the independent variable had little effect on the participants. This is the case if *t* is small. If *t* is large, the two sets of data only partially overlap which means that the independent variable had a (mathematically) noticeable effect on the participants. Put another way, if *t* is small, the null hypothesis (of no difference between the participants' performance in the two conditions) is accepted. If *t* is large, the null hypothesis is rejected. The computation of *t* is usually left to computer software packages; one such multimedia package is the *t-test calculator*.

Specific values of *t* can be converted into a probability, so that the rather vague phrases about extensive and partial overlap used in the previous paragraph, becomes more precise numbers, albeit still probabilities. One value that must be known before you can apply a statistical test is the number of degrees of freedom. Degrees of freedom is an important, if elusive, mathematical term. It is not necessary (or helpful) to know what it means, but usually its numerical value is one less than the number of participants in each condition. (Degrees of freedom is a measure of how many items in a set of data need to be specified before all the items are known. For example, in a two participant trial, if their mean score is 25 and participant 2 scored 18, participant 1 must have scored 32, because no other value would give a mean for the two participants of 25. This trial has 1 degree of freedom.)

The conversion table is Table 1.5. This particular table is valid for data generated from between-participants experimental designs, where each participant provides one datum. Each datum is unaffected by any other datum and so the data are said to be independent. (There are other conversion tables for data generated by other experimental designs, e.g. within-participant designs, where participants provide more than one datum.)

Table 1.5 Critical values of Student's *t*-test for directional and bi-directional hypotheses (i.e. one- and two-tailed tests respectively). Reject the null hypothesis at probability *p* if the calculated value of *t* is equal to, or exceeds, the value in the appropriate row of the table. The degrees of freedom is one less than the number of participants in condition 1, plus one less than the number of participants in condition 2.

Probability, *p*	Directional	0.05	0.025	0.005	0.0005
	Bi-directional		0.05	0.01	0.001
Degrees of freedom					
4		2.13	2.78	4.60	8.61
5		2.02	2.57	4.03	6.87
6		1.94	2.45	3.71	5.96
7		1.89	2.36	3.50	5.41
8		1.86	2.31	3.36	5.04
9		1.83	2.26	3.25	4.78
10		1.81	2.23	3.17	4.59
11		1.80	2.20	3.11	4.44
12		1.78	2.18	3.05	4.32
13		1.77	2.16	3.01	4.22
14		1.76	2.14	2.98	4.14
15		1.75	2.13	2.95	4.07
16		1.75	2.12	2.92	4.01
17		1.74	2.11	2.90	3.97
18		1.73	2.10	2.88	3.92
19		1.73	2.09	2.86	3.88
20		1.72	2.09	2.85	3.85
21		1.72	2.08	2.83	3.82
22		1.72	2.07	2.82	3.79
23		1.71	2.07	2.81	3.77
24		1.71	2.06	2.80	3.75
25		1.71	2.06	2.79	3.73
26		1.71	2.06	2.78	3.71
27		1.70	2.05	2.77	3.69
28		1.70	2.05	2.76	3.67
29		1.70	2.05	2.76	3.66
30		1.70	2.04	2.75	3.65
35		1.69	2.03	2.72	3.59
40		1.68	2.02	2.70	3.55
45		1.68	2.01	2.69	3.52
50		1.68	2.01	2.68	3.50
55		1.67	2.00	2.67	3.48
60		1.67	2.00	2.66	3.46
65		1.67	2.00	2.65	3.45
70		1.67	1.99	2.65	3.43
75		1.67	1.99	2.64	3.42
80		1.66	1.99	2.64	3.42
85		1.66	1.99	2.63	3.41
90		1.66	1.99	2.63	3.40
95		1.66	1.99	2.63	3.40
100		1.66	1.98	2.63	3.39

1.7   The experiment in perspective

This chapter has been primarily concerned with the conduct of the experiment and the analysis of any results. A well-conducted experiment, from which confounding variables have been excluded, is said to have **internal validity**. An experiment, though, is also conducted within a social context and its implication, its **external validity**, should also be considered.

The concepts of statistical reliability, internal validity and external validity can be illustrated with an experiment common in the 1970s. In an attempt to understand the factors controlling aggressive behaviour, a whole series of experiments was conducted using male rats in small boxes with metal grid floors. When a small electric current was passed through the metal floor, the resulting pain caused the rats to attack anything in the box. Numerous experiments investigated the optimum current and voltage to use, the optimum box size and type of floor. Highly statistically reliable results were reported: for instance a current of 0.8 mA was found to provoke reliably more attacks than a current of 0.7 mA in the same box. Many of these experiments had internal validity; they were well conducted and it was possible to draw valid conclusions from them. However, they had little external validity because rats do not normally encounter electric shocks, nor is pain a major initiator of attack.

An experiment is not an isolated event, but takes place within a context. Applying the three concepts of statistical reliability, internal validity and external validity to an experiment puts that experiment into perspective. The outcome of a good experiment is that the experimental hypothesis is valid, beyond reasonable doubt.

1.8   Epilogue

Lots of studies in biological psychology are not experiments, meaning simply that they do not meet the strict criteria of having conditions and an independent variable set out in this book. They may be quasi-experiments, studies of lots of similar case reports, for example, or they may be correlations, but they are not experiments. Such studies are perfectly valid and may be the only way of making any sense of certain information. But when you read such studies, don't spend too long looking for the independent variable and the various conditions – you won't find them.

Experimental design is like plotting a path through a maze. Some routes are definitely wrong (poor design), others are correct but overcomplex (inefficient design). In essence, you must recognize the choices available to you and have a reason for each choice you make.

All studies involve a comparison so, if you are simply repeating a single measure in one situation, you're doing it wrongly. In an experiment you may need to include a control condition in which participants are treated identically to those in your experimental condition except for the independent variable.

You can either do your comparisons between measurements taken from the same participants (within-participants designs) or between measurements taken from different participants (between-participants designs).

Between-participants designs are less efficient because some of the differences between measures must be due to the fact that they are taken from different participants. This means that larger numbers of participants are needed. You also have to be very careful that the conditions are equivalent in everything except the independent variable.

Within-participants designs are more efficient because each participant generates measurements in each condition; it is these measurements which are compared. This is often referred to as participants acting as their own control. Group size can thus be smaller. Within-participants designs have the disadvantage of order effects – after experiencing one condition, the participant may be more practised, fatigued or bored when beginning the second condition. In within-participants designs you must always eliminate order effects by counterbalancing or by randomizing. Note that an individual participant's data are always confounded by an order effect and are thus strictly uninterpretable; only the overall data (from which systematic order effects have been eliminated) make any sense. Within-participants designs are sometimes not possible because experiencing one condition may change the participant in some way, and this may affect their performance in the other condition. This is an example of a transfer or carry-over effect, which in turn is one type of order effect.

The sample of participants you have chosen should be a realistic reflection of the population to which you want to apply your interpretation, so you must check for sampling bias. The experiment itself should be a proper test of the hypotheses, i.e. it should have internal validity; and it would be good if the experiment was relevant to the real world, i.e. it should have external validity. Finally, you should decide whether you need to rule out placebo or experimenter effects by using blind or double-blind procedures.

1.9   Summary of the guide to designing experiments in the behavioural sciences

Experimental design is the art of turning ideas into testable predictions through interventive experiments or non-interventive observations (quasi-experiments). Both these routes involve the measurement of some dependent variable(s). Predictions must be stated precisely and, for statistical analysis, in the form of null and experimental hypotheses. The null hypothesis is always apparently boring and says that nothing happens. In reality, a null result is important because it eliminates a possible field of enquiry. The experimental hypothesis is apparently interesting and says that something happens. In its usual (bi-directional) form it states that things change; in its more restricted (directional) form it states the direction of the change. Observational studies require the measurement and comparison of two (or more) dependent variables, none of which is manipulated (set) by the experimenter. Experimental studies require the measurement and comparison of two (or more) variables, one (or more) of which is the independent variable and is manipulated by the experimenter. The other variables are dependent variables. Testability requires measurement, or sometimes counting, of the dependent variable and a comparison, so more than one variable must be measured, or counted. In experimental studies, manipulation of the independent variable allows causal inference to be made.

The data generated by an experiment have to be analysed using a statistical test. Hence it is necessary to take into account any statistical constraints (e.g. type of data, sample size) that the test imposes before any data are generated.

The hypotheses are couched solely in terms of the dependent variable and, for experimental studies, the independent variable, but there are many other variables.

These cannot all be eliminated so they must be made irrelevant. Typically such variables are controlled, by ensuring that they remain constant as the independent variable changes, or randomized, so that any effects they may have are rendered unsystematic. Essentially, this is to prevent extraneous variables (annoying but relatively harmless) becoming confounding variables (annoying and fatal to the experiment) which vary systematically with the independent variable and provide an alternative explanation of the findings.

Experiments are required to distinguish between changes in a dependent variable caused by an independent variable and changes brought about by chance fluctuations. The null and experimental hypotheses should be carefully stated at the outset, and the dependent variable accurately defined. To draw valid inferences from an experiment there should be no confounding variables. Participants should be carefully selected from a defined population to create a sample and participants from the sample should be randomly allocated to the conditions. The independent variable should be administered and the dependent variable measured without bias and ideally in a double-blind experiment. Data from the conditions of the experiment should be compared using a statistical test and the null hypothesis rejected if the p value is below a particular limit, usually 0.05.

Learning outcomes for Chapter 1

After studying this chapter you should be able to:

1.1 Recognize definitions and applications of each of the terms printed in **bold** in the text.

1.2 Identify and distinguish between independent, dependent, extraneous and confounding variables.

1.3 Recognize statistically reliable results and infer meaning from probability values.

1.4 Identify and state null and experimental hypotheses.

1.5 State the role of the null hypothesis in inferential statistics.

1.6 Understand a normal distribution.

1.7 Comment on the population, sampling and allocation of participants when presented with an experiment.

1.8 State how blind trials reduce experimental bias.

1.9 Justify the choice of within-participant and between-participant experimental designs when designing an experiment.

Questions for Chapter 1

Question 1.1   *(Learning outcome 1.2)*

The general statement 'a warm malted beverage at bedtime promotes sleep' can be tested by experiment. What would be the independent variable and what the dependent variable?

Question 1.2 *(Learning outcome 1.4)*

State one bi-directional and one directional experimental hypothesis of the malted beverage experiment.

Question 1.3 *(Learning outcome 1.2)*

Suppose you designed a malted beverage experiment in which you had one experimental condition and one control condition. State precisely how you would control for the malted beverage.

Question 1.4 *(Learning outcome 1.8)*

In the context of this experiment, what would it mean if it were a randomized double-blind trial?

Question 1.5 *(Learning outcome 1.7)*

The experiment has an independent variable, a dependent variable, it is to be a randomized, double-blind trial, and all necessary extraneous variables have been controlled. What other vital piece of information do you need before you can undertake this experiment?

Question 1.6 *(Learning outcome 1.3, 1.5 and 1.6)*

(a) After analysis, your data reveal a p value of 0.06. What does this mean? (b) How do you know where, on the horizontal axis, to position the graph of a normal distribution?

Question 1.7 *(Learning outcome 1.9)*

An experiment into the effectiveness of positive airway pressure on sleep duration in using participants with breathing difficulties was briefly described in Section 1.5.1. What would be the main advantage and the main disadvantage of using a between-participants design for this experiment?

ANSWERS TO QUESTIONS

Question 1.1

The independent variable would be the warm malted beverage. The experimenter would manipulate this variable by instructing the participant to drink a malted beverage or not to drink a malted beverage at bedtime. The dependent variable is a little more tricky because it has to measure 'sleep promotion'. Here are three possibilities, any one of which would suffice: (1) the dependent variable could be the duration of sleep, measured in minutes; (2) the dependent variable could be some measure of the quality of sleep as reported by the participant upon waking. (The participant would use a predetermined numeric scale of quality devised by the experimenter.); (3) the dependent variable could be the length of time from finishing the drink to falling asleep, that is, the sleep onset latency.

Question 1.2

There are several possible experimental hypotheses, depending on the dependent variable chosen. Assuming the dependent variable is total sleep duration, then the most general bi-directional experimental hypothesis is: 'Drinking a malted beverage at bedtime will affect the duration of the subsequent night's sleep'. Possible directional hypotheses are: 'Drinking a malted beverage at bedtime will increase the duration of the subsequent night's sleep', and 'Drinking a malted beverage at bedtime will reduce the duration of the subsequent night's sleep'.

Question 1.3

The problem here is the possible confounding variable of a beverage. Drinking *anything* just before bed may promote sleep. To control for this possibility, participants should drink a similar quantity of liquid to that consumed by the experimental group. Ideally, the liquid should be the same as the liquid used for the malted beverage (i.e. water or milk). In addition, the temperature of the liquid should be the same in both conditions.

Question 1.4

A randomized trial is one in which either participants have been allocated to conditions on a strictly random basis, or where the order in which participants meet the conditions is done on a strictly random basis. The latter is the most likely. Variation in sleep between individuals is quite large, so the most probable design would be a within-participants design, with participants encountering all conditions. For the trial to be double blind, neither the person administering the beverage and recording sleep duration nor the participant receiving the beverage should know which condition is being administered. (The taste of the beverage and the control liquid can be masked by flavouring both.)

Question 1.5

You would need some information about what participants to use, i.e. about the population to be tested. In particular, their state of health and age would need to be used as defining criteria.

Question 1.6

(a) Strictly the p value is the probability of getting the results by chance, and $p = 0.06$ is quite likely, about 1 in 17. Because the p value is *greater* than 0.05, it means the null hypothesis cannot be rejected and remains a reasonable explanation of the results. (b) The highest point of the graph, which is also the midpoint of the graph, should be located on the horizontal axis at the mean value for the data being plotted.

Question 1.7

The main advantage of using a between-participants design would be the absence of any order effect. The main disadvantage would be the high natural variation in sleep duration between participants.

APPENDIX 1.1
RANDOM NUMBERS

```
20  17  42  28  23  17  59  66  38  61  02  10  86  10  51  55  92  52  44  25
74  49  04  19  03  04  10  33  53  70  11  54  48  63  94  60  94  49  57  38
94  70  49  31  38  67  23  42  29  65  40  88  78  71  37  18  48  64  06  57
22  15  78  15  69  84  32  52  32  54  15  12  54  02  01  37  38  37  12  93
93  29  12  18  27  30  30  55  91  87  50  57  58  51  49  36  12  53  96  40

45  04  77  97  36  14  99  45  52  95  69  85  03  83  51  87  85  56  22  37
44  91  99  49  89  39  94  60  48  49  06  77  64  72  59  26  08  51  25  57
16  23  91  02  19  96  47  59  89  65  27  84  30  92  63  37  26  24  23  66
04  50  65  04  65  65  82  42  70  51  55  04  61  47  88  83  99  34  82  57
32  70  17  72  03  61  66  26  24  71  22  77  88  33  17  78  08  92  73  49

03  64  59  07  42  95  81  39  06  41  20  81  92  34  51  90  39  08  21  42
62  49  00  90  67  86  93  48  31  83  19  07  67  68  49  03  27  47  52  03
61  00  95  36  98  36  14  03  48  88  51  07  33  40  06  86  33  76  68  57
89  03  90  49  28  74  21  04  09  96  60  45  22  03  52  80  01  79  33  81
01  72  33  85  52  40  60  07  06  71  89  27  14  29  55  24  85  79  31  96

27  56  49  79  34  34  32  22  60  53  91  17  33  26  44  70  93  14  99  70
49  05  74  48  10  55  35  25  24  28  20  22  35  66  66  34  26  35  91  23
49  74  37  25  97  26  33  94  42  23  01  28  59  58  92  69  03  66  73  82
20  26  22  43  88  08  19  85  08  12  47  65  65  63  56  07  97  85  56  79
48  87  77  96  43  39  76  93  08  79  22  18  54  55  93  75  97  26  90  77

08  72  87  46  75  73  00  11  27  07  05  20  30  85  22  21  04  67  19  13
95  97  98  62  17  27  31  42  64  71  46  22  32  75  19  32  20  99  94  85
37  99  57  31  70  40  46  55  46  12  24  32  36  74  69  20  72  10  95  93
05  79  58  37  85  33  75  18  88  71  23  44  54  28  00  48  96  23  66  45
55  85  63  42  00  79  91  22  29  01  41  39  51  40  36  65  26  11  78  32
```

ACKNOWLEDGEMENTS

Grateful acknowledgement is made to the following sources for permission to reproduce material in this book:

Figures

Figure 1.1 Data courtesy of Dr Claudio Stampi, Chronobiology Research Institute, Boston, USA.

Every effort has been made to contact copyright holders. If any have been inadvertently overlooked, the publishers will be pleased to make the necessary arrangements at the first opportunity.

Glossary terms are in bold. Italics indicate items mainly, or wholly, in a figure or table.